SERVICES FOR THE ELDERLY

Case Studies in
Administration and Management

Edited by
Milan J. Dluhy & Martha B. Pelaez

SAGE Publications
International Educational and Professional Publisher
Newbury Park   London   New Delhi

For information address:

SAGE Publications, Inc.
2455 Teller Road
Newbury Park, California 91320

SAGE Publications Ltd.
6 Bonhill Street
London EC2A 4PU
United Kingdom

SAGE Publications India Pvt. Ltd.
M-32 Market
Greater Kailash I
New Delhi 110 048 India

Printed in the United States of America

Library of Congress Cataloging-in-Publication Data

Main entry under title:
Services for the elderly : case studies in administration and
    management / edited by Milan J. Dluhy, Martha B. Pelaez.
        p.   cm.
    Includes bibliographical references (p.   ) and index.
    ISBN 0-8039-4409-8 (cl).   —ISBN 0-8039-4410-1 (pb)
        1. Aged—Services for—United States—Management—Case Studies.
    2. Aged—Services for—Government policy—United States—Case
    studies.   I. Dluhy, Milan J., 1942—   . II. Pelaez, Martha B.
    HV1465.S47   1992
    362.6'0973—dc20   92-7395

92 93 94 10 9 8 7 6 5 4 3 2 1

Sage Production Editor: Diane S. Foster

Contents

89613

Foreword

The field of gerontology has made a major effort in the last decade to provide continuing education for professionals in the aging network, and this book is consistent with that effort. This collection of case studies and exercises takes a proven approach, case-based learning, and applies it to issues of organizational development, management, planning, and coordination in the aging field. While the lecture on organizational theory, public administration, and business administration has focused on these kinds of issues for many years, there has been a paucity of attention paid to these issues in the aging field. Professionals in aging will find that these case studies deal with real, day-to-day issues. The cases, although hypothetical exercises, are cases that have already been field tested with professionals. Therefore, the reader will find the issues presented in the cases very familiar. The problems and dilemmas presented in the cases are the challenges facing most professionals in the aging field today.

Each case included in this book was developed and field tested under a grant from the U.S. Administration on Aging during 1985 and 1986. The case methodology discussed in the Introduction demonstrates the care the authors have taken in developing the case studies so that they would be a great utility to professionals.

The Southeast Florida Center on Aging at Florida International University is pleased to have sponsored and directed the project that produced the cases that are included in this book. It is my hope that future projects in which the Center will participate will continue to contribute to the development of high-quality educational materials for professionals in the aging field.

Max B. Rothman, J. D.
Executive Director
Southeast Florida Center on Aging,
Florida International University

Preface

In 1985 the Southeast Florida Center on Aging at Florida International University and the Miami Jewish Home for the Aged applied for and received a U.S. Administration on Aging grant to develop and then field test a case-based learning program for personnel in the aging network. The case studies appearing in this book were developed and tested under this grant. Since the end of the grant period, the cases have been widely used throughout the state of Florida within the aging network. The cases are generic to the field of aging and have broad applicability. The settings, issues, and types of agencies and organizations portrayed in these cases are similar to those in the aging network throughout the U.S. in design and purpose. These cases have broad applicability to the following personnel:

1. Managers and supervisors of community-based elderly service programs such as adult day-care centers, senior activity centers, senior meal sites, home-health services, and home-delivered meals.
2. Direct service personnel in elderly care programs such as nurses and social workers who are interested in increasing their administrative and management skills.
3. Managers and supervisors of long-term care facilities.

4. Managers, supervisors, program staff, and training staff of Area Agencies on Aging and state and local program offices on aging, which oversee government-funded aging programs.

5. Local government employees involved in the planning, development, delivery, and assessment of long-term care and other services for the elderly.

6. Students enrolled in professional degree programs in social gerontology, social work, health-services administration, public administration, and business administration.

These audiences are the primary target for the use of the cases included in this book. The cases incorporate the thinking of various faculty members from the university and of experienced professionals in the aging field. The objective of this book is to provide the aging network with practical cases for the training and development of executives in agencies and programs serving the older population.

                                                        Martha B. Pelaez

Acknowledgments

We would like to thank JoAnne Bander and Irma Emery of the Stein Gerontological Institute of the Miami Jewish Home and Hospital for the Aged for interviewing directors and supervisors of agencies and programs serving the older adult and for developing case vignettes.

We would also like to thank the authors and the following group leaders for their assistance in field testing *Cases in Elderly Services:*

NANCY ALLEN
Special Programs Coordinator, Dade County CAA

BARBARA REITZ
Administrative Assistant, Miami Jewish Home and Hospital for the Aged

SISTER PEGGY WHITENECK
Director of Mission Services, Bon Secours Hospital, Villa Maria Nursing Home

SHERRY TUCKER
Operations Manager, Mae Volen Senior Center

JUNE MICHEL
Executive Director, Mae Volen Senior Center

JENNIFER BELT
President, Elder Interest Fund

HOWARD RUSSELL
Administrator of Impact Program, Metro-Dade Elderly Services

MARY GUTHRIE
Director, Home Care Services, Channeling Project, Miami Jewish
Home and Hospital for the Aged

Introduction

Milan J. Dluhy

Martha B. Pelaez

The statistics about older Americans are well known today, and the public has begun to incorporate into their view of the future the fact that our population will continue to become older well into the next century. People 65 years and over number 31.0 million (1989), and this represents 12.5% of the U.S. population or about one in every eight Americans. Projections indicate that when the "baby boom" generation reaches 65 between the years 2010 and 2030, our population over 65 will jump to 65 million or two and one-half times the number in 1980. At this rate the percentage of older people will climb to 21.2% by 2030 or one in every five Americans (American Association of Retired People). As the population distribution has become more skewed in the direction of the elderly, the aging network that provides services to this population group has grown by leaps and bounds. As Brown (1983) indicates:

> The term aging network is used to connote the totality of agencies, organizations, interest groups, service providers, and management and professional staff that is broadly concerned with aging policy, services, and program development. . . . This network includes fifty-seven units, over six hundred area agencies, and nearly twelve thousand nutrition sites. (p. 204)

This book is primarily written for those professionals and other workers in agencies and organizations that are part of the aging network and that were largely spawned and continue to be funded under the Older Americans Act of 1965. This set of agencies and organizations have some common characteristics that will be discussed later, but of central significance is the fact that the personnel who have the responsibility for delivering services and programs throughout the aging network are known to have a major need for additional training and continuing education in administration and management (Southeast Florida Center on Aging, 1985). The need for additional executive-level training and education will further the trend toward "professionalism" evident in the aging field (Vinyard, 1983).

While the primary emphasis among service providers in the 1970s appeared to be developing enough services to meet the varied needs of the elderly so that a continuum of services was in place, the 1980s was concerned primarily with improving coordination of existing services, channeling individuals into services that best meet their needs and developing common intake and case-management systems at the local level (Gelfand, 1988). The 1990s will be concerned with reduced budgets, the need for targeting services, and expanding community-based long-term care services as a less costly alternative to nursing homes (Weissert, Cready, & Pawelak, 1988). These changes in the service-delivery system for the elderly have demanded executives who not only understand the clients and their needs, but who also understand how to link and connect the different parts of the aging network while keeping their individual agencies and organizations abreast of the changing fiscal environment. In short, the executives in the aging field today are being asked to do much more than just build a new program and get it operating successfully. They are being asked to move from an approach that in the past stressed the building and then maintenance of an existing bureaucracy to an approach that stresses development where new organizations are created out of old ones, where decision making is used as a change process, and where adapting to an ever-changing external environment is absolutely essential (Brown, 1983). In light of this gradual evolution of the aging network to accommodate the changing needs of the ever-increasing number of elderly population, it is critical that the administrative and management problems with which executives struggle regularly in the aging field be addressed and that useful educational materials be developed so that ongoing executive development can continue.

The Literature on Administration and Management in Aging

Surprisingly, there is no identifiable body of literature on administration and management in the aging field. (A few exceptions are Brown, 1983; Estes & Newcomer, 1983; and Kutza, 1984). While there is some helpful literature in the specialized and narrow area of nursing home administration, there has been virtually no attention in the literature paid directly to executives in the aging network. As a result, executives in the aging network who are interested in administration and management have had to turn to literature in the more general fields of human services, public administration, and business and health care administration. One of the consequences of turning to the more general fields of administration and management is that the literature has been recently dominated by themes such as cutback management and retrenchment budgeting, strategic planning, and marketing of services.

For example, a computerized search of titles in the administration and management field reveals the following:

- "Doing More with Less" (Turem & Born, 1983)
- "Managing the Human Services in Hard Times" (Bresnick, 1983)
- "Cost Effectiveness of Alternative Strategies for Cutback Management" (Greenhalgh & McKersie, 1980)
- "Strategic Planning Under Current Cutback Conditions" (McLaughlin, 1982)
- "Managing Human Service Organizations with Limited Resources" (Knighton & Heidelman, 1984)
- "Meshing Human Resources Planning with Strategic Business Planning" (Baird, Meshoulam, & DeGive, 1983)
- "Social Planning in an Environment of Limited Choice" (Capoccia & Googins, 1982)
- "Marketing Home Health Care to the Rural Elderly" (Lancaster, 1988).

The more salient point, however, is that the content of the literature in administration and management recently has been focused on what organizations and agencies can do when resources are severely limited. The executives in the aging network have not experienced the degree of resource constraints that many other organizations and agencies have in the broader field of human services and government (Estes & Newcomer, 1983). Aging network executives have been building programs in the last decade and, therefore, the cutback management, strategic planning, and marketing literature has been of only limited utility. Consequently the lack of specialized knowledge for executives in the aging field and the preoccupation of the general administration and management literature with resource constraint issues has left executives in the aging network searching for timely and relevant information that can be used for executive development purposes.

The Environment of the Aging Network Executive

A brief review of the environment in which the aging network executive has been operating in during the past decade will give some insight into the types of issues and problems that these executives have been facing and, therefore, the areas that should be targeted for executive-level development and training, the focus of this volume.

The Reagan Administration, beginning in 1981, dealt a severe blow to many of the programs in the human services. The standard theme of the first four years of the Administration was retrenchment budgets for most domestic program areas and modest increases for military spending (Palmer & Sawhill, 1984). Where major budget cuts did not take place, the emphasis was on cost containment and limiting further program growth. The domestic program areas that were the hardest hit were urban development, anti-poverty programs, transportation, and new subsidized housing construction. In contrast, programs impacting on the elderly did not experience the same level of budget cuts that other domestic program areas felt. In fact, as Table 1 illustrates for the years 1980 through 1989, the Older Americans Act funded

Table 1. Federal Outlays for Selected Health, Housing, and Social Services for the Elderly, 1980-1989

Program	1980	1981	1982	1983	1984	1985	1986	1987	1988	1989	Notes
Administration on Aging Programs Under OAA Act *	647	669	635	671	689	701	671	726	725	701	Older Americans Act of 1965
Social Services Block Grant Program **	2.3	2.6	2.5	2.5	2.8	2.8	2.7	2.7	2.7	2.7	Formerly called Title XX
Medicare Hospital Insurance Trust Fund **	24.2	29.2	34.8	38.8	42.3	48.7	49.7	50.8	52.5	54.8	Medicare Part-A Hospital
Medicare Federal Supplementary Medical Insurance Trust Fund **	10.7	13.2	15.6	18.8	20.4	22.7	26.2	30.8	35.1	39.7	Medicare Part-B Physician Fees
Medicaid **	14.5	16.8	17.3	18.9	20.0	22.7	25.0	27.4	30.6	32.7	Only Includes Federal Shares
Section 202 Direct Loan Program *	742	817	742	799	661	501	531	404	545	530	Only for Elderly and Handicapped
HUD Subsidized Housing Programs **	4.5	5.7	6.8	7.8	8.8	10.0	10.1	10.0	10.1	12.4	Includes Section 8 & Public Housing rent subsidies

SOURCE: Budget of the U.S. Government, Fiscal Years 1982-1989. Appendices. Government Printing Office: Washington, D.C.
NOTES: * Amount shown in millions.
         ** Amount shown in billions.

programs actually increased modestly, the Social Services Block Grant program stayed about the same, Medicare and Medicaid grew substantially, and subsidies to existing low- to moderate-income housing projects continued to increase slowly. Only the Section 202 program, which provided direct loans for construction of new housing for the elderly and handicapped, was gradually curtailed during this period. These figures suggest that while programs aimed at the elderly did not experience a windfall, neither did they experience serious shortfalls. A better characterization of the fiscal environment for the major programs within the aging network is that after factoring in inflation, aging programs at least held their own or maintained a constant level of budget support. In fact, in the health care area, there was substantial growth. It would be more accurate to describe the fiscal environment as stagnant in some areas and growing in other areas when it comes to federal funding.

Reports from the states also indicate that during this period the elderly fared better than most other population groups when it came to fiscal support for their programs. Other areas within the human services appear to have taken the brunt of the budget cuts (Austin, 1984; Dluhy & Rothman, 1986; and Estes & Newcomer, 1983). If fiscal conditions worsen in the 1990s, however, it is possible that elderly programs may no longer be protected from deep cuts and resource constraints.

As one analyst reminds us, the elderly have substantial public support within the population that translates into political support for programs aimed largely at them (Brown, 1983). On the other hand, it is also the case that the argument that the elderly are getting a disproportionate share of society's resources is beginning to take hold within political circles and among some segments of the general population, and this suggests that in the future advocates for the elderly may increasingly be forced to defend existing policies and programs rather than suggesting new or expanded initiatives (Vinyard, 1983).

In summary, the fiscal environment in the 1980s has not created the degree of fiscal constraints in the aging network that it has in other human-service areas. Because government funding has tightened considerably compared to the 1960s and 1970s, however, *executives in the aging network would be wise to develop skills that allow them to develop more nongovernment sources of funding as well as to modify their programs to accommodate a fiscal environment that is now emphasizing such things as fund raising, grantsmanship, client fees, sliding-fee scales, and using volunteers in place of paid staff.* These are the realities facing the aging network executives today. The major characteristic of the fiscal environment in the 1990s is that executives in the aging network can continue to assume in the short run that their government support base will remain stable, but if they want to pursue additional funds for new services or they want expansion of existing services, they will have to be very creative, strategic, and entrepreneurial in seeking out nongovernment resources (Dluhy, 1986).

Aging programs are embedded in a federal system that can be described as decentralized, dominated by jurisdictional sprawl and fragmented power, and one where there has been a demonstrated avoidance of concentrated authority (Brown, 1983). Because the Older Americans Act passed in 1965 established a three-tiered arrangement in which authority and funding were distributed among federal, state, and local agencies and because this system of services has relied on the nonprofit or voluntary sector for the most part to actually deliver services, the environment for program administration has been extremely complex. The diversity, fragmentation, and specialization of services in the aging network requires executives to regularly deal with problems of coordination, the pooling of different funding sources, and coalition building for advocacy purposes. The agency environment is fluid and loosely organized and the successful executive must be able to manage a complex interorganizational environment that is constantly changing.

In this respect the political aspects of administration are becoming more salient than the technical competence to deliver a particular service (Perlmutter, 1986). Here the major point is that skills related to the management of the external environment of the agency or organization are very much needed by executives in addition to the more traditional skills needed for the internal day-to-day management of agencies or organizations.

Finally, many of the agencies and organizations in the aging network who actually deliver services can be characterized as small to medium in size (fewer than 100 employees), having executives without a great deal of formal training in administration and management, having multiple sources of funding, and being governed by boards composed of local citizens (Dluhy & Rothman, 1986; Estes & Newcomer, 1983; see Chapter 10). These agencies and organizations are not large, highly bureaucratized, and staffed with administrators and managers trained in the most advanced management techniques. Rather, the profile in the aging network is one of community-based programs that struggle in a highly uncertain fiscal environment. They often turn to executives who may be recruited from direct service or who are switching over from another field or profession. At the present time the nonprofit or voluntary organizations that are the mainstay of the delivery system in the aging network are in much need of executive-level development and training, especially in the challenges associated with managing a highly complex external environment.

The cases in this book reflect the reality of the 1990s for executives in the aging network. Expansion of services to fill out the continuum of care and seeking alternative sources of nongovernmental funding will necessitate executives to be skilled in a wide variety of areas. However, this changing fiscal environment in the future indicates that executives will need skill in areas such as: adapting their agency's mission to the new fiscal environment, working carefully with their boards to develop new sources of funding and marketing their services in the community successfully, adapting their agency internally to external change, managing multiple sources of government and nongovernment funding, evaluating the outcomes of their programs more clearly, and building coalitions in their communities to secure more resources and develop new programs.

The Case Study Approach for Training Executives

The need for educational materials for executive development and training within the aging network has been identified as critical. There has been little written that directly addresses the administrative and management problems that frequently face executives in the network. Because of the major changes that have occurred within the external environment that executives have been working in over the last decade, it has been argued that these executives are currently most in need of educational and training materials that focus on external management issues. For the time being, skill development in the external management area is a high priority (Austin, 1984). Materials on internal management issues and especially cutback management issues are more readily available in the literature. Accordingly, this book focuses on cases that will permit executives to sharpen their problem-solving skills in areas that will allow them to focus on the continued development of their agencies or organizations.

In this context, the cases focus on skills that will allow executives to look toward the future by finding new sources of nongovernment funding, by enhancing their ability to deal with the political aspects of administration as opposed to the technical aspects of running a bureaucracy, by furthering their ability to manage complex interagency organizational environments, and, most important, by helping executives develop the capacity to be creative, entrepreneurial, and above all "strategic planners."

The executive of today in the aging network is far more than a technician and far more than a good fund raiser. Successful executives must also be able to adroitly manage their external environment and allow their agency or organization to adapt to this ever-changing environment by helping their staffs and boards to improve decision making so that they can strategically change and modify their goals and objectives to accommodate the aging population of today and tomorrow.

The case study approach is a well-known and proven method for training executives in business and public administration (Yin, 1984). Case studies that stress problem-solving approaches to critical organizational issues allow executives in the field to learn by being exposed to a structured learning environment that stresses interaction among experienced executives who need insight into concepts, approaches, and techniques that work well in dynamic organizational settings. The learning is highly experiential in nature and is well suited to the busy executive who does not have the time and interest in taking a course or series of seminars for an extended period of time.

As the methodology in the next section explains, these cases are composites of many situations rather than a true account of what actually happened in any given situation. These cases were developed for teaching purposes and, therefore, their purpose was simply to establish a framework for discussion. Using this as background, the following steps were used to develop and test the case studies.

CASE METHODOLOGY

To make the case materials realistic and to approximate the type of day-to-day problems that executives in the aging network face, the methodology used to develop the cases involved personnel from the network at every step of case development and refinement. There were three critical stages for developing the cases.

Initially, 21 aging network personnel in South Florida were selected to represent a wide range of community-based and institutional agencies and organizations within the network. These individuals came from a range of backgrounds that included Bachelor's degree in a liberal arts subject to Master's degree in social work and business. Each person was interviewed about his or her agency or organization as well as those problems he or she could identify within the aging field. They were asked, among other things, to talk about their agency in terms of historical development, mission and goals, organization and financial structure, client populations served, services provided, backgrounds of staff and, *most importantly, the frequent and recurring problems they encountered in administration and management.* These interviews were transcribed for background purposes for the next stage in the process.

An interdisciplinary team was selected to proceed with recommendations and summaries from the interviews. This team included project staff on the grant and university faculty chosen to write the cases. Based on the interview summaries, eight draft cases were written. (Only seven of these initial cases are included in this book because one of the cases proved to be too difficult to use based on field tests.) After the faculty had written the draft cases, 85 practitioners from the aging network were invited to a two- hour session to review the cases and make helpful suggestions about the content included in each case in terms of its utility for other personnel in the network. This focus group, plus informal interviews with some of the more active participants, served as input to the faculty, who then revised the drafts of the cases.

After completion of the revisions, 70 practitioners (different from the first group but also drawn from the aging network) were invited to participate in a series of workshops where each of the cases was presented. For all practical purposes, these three stages resulted in the final case products appearing in this book. The final cases were also used on three different occasions in 1987-1988 with executives from the aging network. The positive response received from executives who actually used the case materials for development and training purposes was one of the central reasons that these cases are presented in book form so that they could be used widely within the aging network. At all stages of development, the actual cases were written to be as generic as possible for the aging network. They do not, in the judgment of the project staff, the faculty who wrote them, or the participants who gave their input about the content of the cases, represent situations just limited to Florida. The problems in the external environment described earlier are ones that agencies and organizations have faced throughout the country.

HOW TO USE THE CASES

The seven cases in the book can be used in many different ways, and a creative executive, local Area Agency, state office, or even a professional association can set up continuing-education programs for using these cases for professional development. We believe, however, that the best results can be achieved by following the steps recommended below:

1. Start by dealing with one case at a time, but we recommend that in the course of the training, all seven cases should be used. Read the introduction to each case. This provides a brief summary of the key concepts used in each case.

2. Have each participant in the session fill out the pretest given along with each case.

3. Have each participant read the case in its entirety. Ask them to take a piece of paper and identify the basic issues about which decisions need to be made in the case. Ask them to also write down a few possible solutions and to evaluate the strengths and weaknesses of each solution. Stress that there is no right answer.

4. Next comes group discussion of the case. The group leader or trainer should use the questions and the discussion of these questions included at the end of each case to help the participants during the group discussion. The group leader should try to develop consensus wherever possible and should encourage more discussion where there is less agreement. Usually 90 minutes for discussion is sufficient.

5. Finally, ask participants to fill out the posttest and then spend approximately 20 to 30 minutes discussing what they learned from the case and how it relates to their work situation. All together an approximate time frame might be:

    Introduction, instructions, pretest: 10 minutes
    Read case: 30 minutes
    Discussion: 90 minutes
    Posttest, wrap up: 30 minutes
    Total training time per case: 160 minutes or 2 hours
       and 40 minutes.

A brief summary of the external environment and seven cases included in the book will provide the reader with an overview of the book.

SUMMARY Of CASE STUDIES

The hypothetical state in these cases is not only one of the fastest-growing states in the Sunbelt, but also the continued heavy in-migration of retired people has made the state a showcase for the rest of the country in terms of how an increasingly aging society will evolve. Of particular interest is the fact that while elderly retirees still continue to come to the state in large numbers, many elderly are also returning to their states of origin, especially when physical, mental, and financial problems become unmanageable for them. The statistics show that the state as a whole has gained 350,000 people over the age of 60 during the last five years. (This is after those migrating out have been subtracted from those migrating in.) In short, the state's elderly population is projected to reach 24% of the state's total population by the year 2000.

Lime County follows the overall demographic patterns of the state, except that the net population gains are more modest. Specifically, Lime County has had a net gain of 5,000 people over 60 years of age in the last five years. Analysis by the Area Agency on Aging further reveals that in-migrants are generally younger, healthier, and more economically secure than those leaving the state. However, there is still a significant segment of the population that remains in Lime County that is over 80, frail, and living at or below the poverty level. This "at-risk" group is also disproportionately Hispanic and black. The picture, then, is one of affluent and healthy elderly coming in, some elderly leaving, and a significant number of elderly already in the county moving into the "at-risk" category. Estimates are that this "at-risk" group will increase by 50% each decade through the year 2010. In numerical terms, the county expects to have 10,000 more "at- risk" elderly by the turn of the century and 20,000 more by 2010. This "at-risk" category will need help of all kinds, and the county is bracing for an increased demand for services.

Lime County is both multiethnic and multiracial. As of 1988, 35% of the elderly were black, 22% were Hispanic, 5% were Jewish, and 38% were nonminority and white. Estimates are that the black and Hispanic elderly population will continue to grow in numbers, while the Jewish and nonminority white elderly population will continue to shrink in numbers.

The county has a diverse set of agencies and service providers. The United Way indicates that there are 105 distinct nonmedical social service agencies serving the elderly in the county. Many of these agencies service specific geographic areas and, as a result, serve well-identified racial or ethnic target groups. Other agencies have a more mixed clientele. While there are a few large agencies with budgets in the millions of dollars and staffs that are highly professionalized, most of the agencies are small, rely heavily on volunteers, and survive from year to year on small budgets. There is a lot of competition between agencies for resources and, in some cases, competition for the same clients. It is quite difficult to get agencies to cooperate on issues of mutual concern since each must protect its turf if it is to survive. Recent program cuts in Washington will exacerbate the problem since many agencies are likely to take two or three successive annual cuts in their budgets. Therefore survival for many is critical, and most thoughtful observers in the county think that joint agreements, more coordination, mergers, and outright agency closings will be more common than ever before because of the fiscal environment.

The service providers in the county formed a council a number of years ago to discuss issues of mutual concern. The council now has 60 members who meet regularly to share information and concerns. Besides the 105 nonmedical agencies serving the elderly, there are nine major community-based hospitals, five active health maintenance organizations, a medical school and complex, and two gerontological centers. The county is indeed complex, and the fear is that many elderly are still either underserved or unserved by the existing institutions and agencies. *The most pressing concern here is how this community can go about solving its problems—that is, how problems get identified, how organizations network to examine these problems, and how interagency cooperation is accomplished to solve the problems.* In a dynamic community like Lime County, there is always the fear that the problems and needs of the elderly have become secondary to the agendas and programs of the existing agencies and institutions in the community. Even though Lime County is dynamic and changing, there is a real need for this community to develop an ability to respond to the emerging and critical needs of the elderly.

1. *Keeping Your Agency Mission Current*

This case presents a situation that requires management to reformulate its planning. Participants are asked to contrast two different mission statements, to understand the difference between long-range and strategic planning, to examine changes in the external environment and note viable strategies for adjusting to this environment, to identify and discuss long-range objectives for a geriatric center, and to examine the process for formulating a 5-10 year strategic plan.

2. *Board Development*

This case presents a multiservice, multifunded organization providing leisure time activities and nutrition services to the poor and frail elderly of the county. Due to sudden changes in funding and leadership, the board becomes a key factor in the agency's survival. Participants are asked to develop a set of goals and objectives for a human services agency board, to identify desirable characteristics, skills, and qualifications of potential board members, and to identify the qualities necessary in the executive-management function of a multiservice agency serving elderly citizens.

3. Marketing Elderly Services

This case presents a nursing home with an in-home service program for the frail elderly funded by a foundation's grant. Unless this program is marketed successfully, it cannot be continued after the initial grant money is exhausted. Participants are asked to examine a preliminary marketing plan, to critique it, and to offer recommendations for both expanding and strengthening it.

4. Managing Change

This case presents a church-affiliated community-based service program offering housing, home-delivered meals, adult day-care center and a homemaker service program to a low-income black population. The church membership decides to reduce its financial commitment to these projects and request that they become a separate not-for-profit corporation. Participants are asked to analyze organizational conflicts, give specific strategies to implement planned change, and discuss management approaches to problem-solving.

5. Fiscal Accountability

This case presents a multiservice, multifunded elderly services organization with a major cash-flow problem. Participants are asked to discuss the dilemmas associated with the failure of a funding agency to fund a program in a timely manner, to examine some of the ways of handling a cash-flow problem, to recommend a course of action for resolving a program facing a shortfall, and to set forth a strategy for dealing with recurring cash-flow problems.

6. *Evaluating Program Effectiveness*

This case presents a county elderly services program that has been running very successfully under the leadership of a dynamic director who was able to secure a five-year foundation grant. Before the three-year evaluation report is due, the director dies. Participants are asked to identify the key aspects of program evaluation and to design an evaluation process for the three years of activities funded by the foundation grant.

7. *The Dynamics of Coalition Building*

This case presents a fast-growing county that is both multi-ethnic and multiracial with a diverse set of agencies and service providers. Most of the agencies are small and survive from year-to-year on small budgets. There is a lot of competition among agencies for resources and, in some cases, competition for the same clients. Participants are asked to identify the essential elements of successful coalitions, to recognize different types of coalitions, and to understand the effective management of an established coalition.

1

Keeping Your Agency Mission Current

INTRODUCTION   Elliot J. Stern

CASE STUDY   Richard M. Hodgetts

Introduction

On the face of it, a mission statement would seem a simple thing to develop for an organization. After all, if you do not know the purpose of your organization, it becomes very difficult to develop concrete goals and objectives, realistic action plans and appropriate community support. Yet the development of a brief statement of purpose of an organization—especially in times when human-service organizations must respond to changing community needs, diminishing sources of support, and new community perceptions about their roles and functions—can become one of the most critical activities for any organization.

This case is particularly concerned with the relationship of your agency's mission to its long- and short-range planning process and the concrete action steps it must attain to achieve its central purpose.

It is by now well established that organizations that engage in realistic long- and short-range planning outperform agencies who do not, even when these plans are not fully actualized or successfully completed. The foundation for any successful long-range plan is the development of a succinct and central statement of purpose around which organizations can define their identity and, in turn, be perceived by other private and public agencies, including potential sources of funding and continuing support, as in control of their destiny and cognizant of what it takes to achieve their objectives.

The case itself is not a resource for understanding the complete long-range and strategic planning processes. Rather, it focuses on the concrete questions involved in beginning a strategic planning process. When do the capabilities of the organization and the demands of its social, economic, and service environment require a restatement of its central purpose? How can the meaning of contrasting mission statements be related to institutional self-definition and organization for planning purposes as well as community awareness. We believe that one of the prerequisites to developing a long-range plan is to understand the realities that affect operations including its strengths, weaknesses, challenges, and opportunities.

The mission posits statement is the reason of the organization. It is central for communicating organizational intent clearly, both inside and outside the organization. The clearer and more concise this statement is, the greater its utility for planning purposes. The next step is the planning process, including setting up goals and objectives, strategic development, resource allocation; and specific work loads and assignments follow from it. When developed with appropriate input from staff and board, with additional reality testing by informal comments or reviews from outside, the planning process can enable an organization to be continually monitored and managed in terms of a set of clearly defined performance criteria.

Review this case as one that requires a reformulation of the planning process so that organizational objectives can be clearly set forth and self-correcting procedures can be implemented that will enable an organization to understand its purpose and to measure its own effectiveness.

The Changing Environment:
A Case in Strategic Planning

Pleasant Manor is a comprehensive geriatric center. The center was founded in 1937 under the sponsorship of the Presbyterian churches. After giving the matter a great deal of thought, the founding board agreed on the following mission statement:

> Pleasant Manor is hereby established to provide a comfortable residence for older people who need a group living environment. We are committed to providing a comfortable home in the Christian tradition for such older citizens. To this end we have founded Pleasant Manor as a retirement home for older people.

The initial facility was a 15-unit structure. However, between 1937 and 1970 dramatic increases took place in the county's overall population. This was accompanied by a large increase in the number of elderly people in the area. In 1937 only 2% of the county's residents were 65 or older. By 1970 that number had mushroomed to 15%. As this developing trend became evident to the trustees, the board made a number of decisions regarding expansion of the facilities. In 1945 the home's size was doubled to accommodate 30 beds. In 1954 an additional 40 beds were added, and in 1958 a third increase brought the overall total to 100 beds. The 1960s were boom years for the county and, once again, the trustees responded with a dynamic brick-and-mortar strategy. By 1970 Pleasant Manor was a 200-bed skilled nursing facility.

The 1970s also saw a continued increase in the county's overall population. The 1980 census reported that there were now just more than 500,000 people in the county. Based on calculations made by the administrator of Pleasant Manor, the number of persons 65 years of age or older in the county had risen from 33,000 in 1970 to approximately 50,000 in 1980. This meant that the percentage of the county population in this age category had risen from 9.7% to 10.6%.

During the 1970s new sources of government money became available for those providing community-based programs for elderly people. As a result, Pleasant Manor was able to provide additional services to the elderly, including a home-delivered meals program, an adult day-care center, an adult congregate living facility for individuals who need some support services but not the skilled care of a nursing home, and a homemaker service program.

CURRENT SITUATION

The last 5 years have seen a major change in demographic trends in the area. At first the change was not noticeable, but by 1983 federal and county statistics began to present a clear picture of what Pleasant Manor could look forward to during the decade 1985-1995. The major development was that while the overall population of the county would continue to grow, the retiree population was no longer increasing. The number of new retirees entering the area and the number of residents reaching retirement age was decreasing. Also, many of those in the 55-65 age category were moving to adjacent counties because land prices and the general cost of living were lower there. One individual, who had recently moved to an adjacent county, explained his reasoning this way:

> Thanks to the influx of a number of new high-tech businesses, this area is growing fast. These companies are attracting younger people (30-45 years of age), people with young families. The young people have plenty of money to spend and that's driving prices up. I simply can't compete with these people. I'm 58 years old, and when I retire in 7 years my pension won't give me the same purchasing power I can get by moving to the next county. With prices so attractive here, I can sell my house for five times what I paid for it 25 years ago and buy a similar one 30 miles away for less than 70% of the sales price of my old house.

During the last 3 years the population trend has become more pronounced. The latest county data portrays a developing "population gap." The number of people between the ages of 40-55 continues to increase. The number between 56-70 is declining. The number 71 and over is increasing rapidly. To further confirm the accuracy of these figures, the administrator of Pleasant Manor recently reported that he has been inundated with telephone calls and letters from adjacent counties asking for advice about what they can do to provide services to the recent influx of retirees.

Last month the president of the board of trustees and the administrator decided that it was time to take a look at the center's plan for the next decade. In the past, Pleasant Manor has not spent a great deal of time studying trends in the external environment or analyzing how these would affect the center. Most of the planning has consisted of estimating the number of elderly people who would be in the county during the next 12-24 months and determining the types of services that these people would need. Now it is obvious that basing a plan on the assumption that the future will just be an encore of the past will not work.

In responding to recent developments, the board has decided to do two things. First, it will rethink its basic mission and rewrite its mission statement. Second, it will formulate a strategic plan that will ensure the continuance of Pleasant Manor as a quality geriatric center at the forefront as a provider of comprehensive care to the elderly through both institutional and community services.

MANAGEMENT'S VIEW

The chairman of the board and the administrator will both be playing key roles in these two major steps described in the above paragraph. In fact, both will have to work in close harmony if the center is to survive. The local newspaper recently learned of the situation at Pleasant Manor and sent a reporter out to interview both men. Here is what each had to say:

Chairman   We've done an excellent job of providing quality care to the elderly in the community for almost half a century, and we intend to go on doing this. However, for the first time since we can remember there has been a shift in the retired population and we find ourselves with an increasing number of people 71 or more years of age. In fact, believe it or not, more than 42% of the people to whom we are providing service are 85 years or older. This means that the services we used to provide will have to be changed to meet current needs. Five years ago only 12% of our clients were over 85. The bottom line is: better planning. It's a challenge, but one that I know we're going to be able to meet.

Administrator   For the last 50 years, and certainly for the last 10 that I've been here, we've been able to carry out what I call straight-line extrapolation planning. By figuring out how many older people we had in this county and how many would be moving in we could very easily figure out what types of services we needed to offer. However, this isn't the case anymore. This county is no longer the retirement community it once was. Our neighbors to the west and the south are gaining population in the 55-70 age category while we're losing. A lot of the services we currently provide are for people in this age category. So we are not geared toward handling so many older people over the age of 80. In short, our client population is changing. Now we have to develop a strategic plan for adjusting to this new market.

Specifically, this means a new mission statement, objectives, and a plan for coping with this new environment. Like the chairman said, "it's going to be a challenge, but I know we're up to the task."

LATEST DEVELOPMENTS

At its meeting earlier this week, the management of the Pleasant Manor took the first step toward developing a strategic plan. A new mission statement was formulated. The new mission states:

Pleasant Manor is a skilled nursing care center serving the elderly of this county. It is dedicated to providing quality care in a Christian environment for all elders needing service. Wherever possible, it will seek alternatives to nursing home care for the elderly citizens it serves while providing a comfortable residence for those who require nursing home care.

The board is now preparing a detailed strategic plan. Included in this plan will be objectives and services to be offered in the future. The administrator would particularly like to have the plan address the possibility of some cooperative relationship with centers in adjoining counties that do not have all of the facilities or services that Pleasant Manor now offers. "Perhaps we can work out an arrangement whereby we can help them out," he said. "After all, we know a lot more about providing services to the elderly than any of them do. We've been in this business for 50 years." The other members of the board agree, but would like to focus first on what the strategic plan should look like and how this plan can help the Manor meet its new basic mission.

Questions for Discussion

1. What are the major factors that necessitate a change in an organization's mission?
2. How should an organization approach changing its mission? Who should be involved in making changes to the mission? What process should be used?
3. How can strategic planning help in changing an organization's mission?
4. What process should an organization use to facilitate strategic planning?
5. Who should be involved in the strategic planning process? Who are the key stakeholders?

Pretest/Posttest

Answer each question T or F (True or False)

T 1. A mission statement contains an organization's long-range objectives.

F 2. Mission statements never change, regardless of changes in the external environment.

T 3. Population changes are one of the key factors to consider in health care planning.

F 4. A strategic plan and a long-range plan are the same thing.

F 5. Strategic objectives focus on efficiency; operational objectives focus on effectiveness.

T 6. Strategic plans place a strong emphasis on changes in the external environment.

T 7. Over the last 10 years, health care organizations have come to realize that strategic planning is a critical phase of their overall management process.

T   8. Strategic and operational objectives are linked together
          in the strategic planning process.

T   9. Over the last 30 years the basic mission statement of
          many health care organizations have changed dramat-
          ically.

T   10. One of the biggest problems in strategic planning is that
          continual changes in the external environment require
          changes in the plan.

2

Board Development

INTRODUCTION   Milan J. Dluhy

CASE STUDY   Sanford L. Kravitz

Introduction

The importance of working with your agency board is often overlooked in most discussions of the central tasks of executives and administrators of organizations. Among other things, agency boards provide legitimacy in the community for the programs delivered by the agency; they establish and articulate the organization's mission; and they give the organization access to a wide range of community resources. Adroit executives learn early to nurture their boards. The tendency by many is to see boards as largely symbolic in nature, but as this case illustrates, boards need not be confined to this rather superficial and limited role. Instead, boards have the capacity to help the executive lead the organization and provide the energy and vision needed to keep the organization on a clear path.

Executives, once they have taken their boards seriously, have the job of making sure that the right kind of people are selected, that these people are properly oriented to the organization and its services, and that the Board meets regularly and is involved in the development of a meaningful agenda. It is well established that task-centered groups such as agency boards can be efficient tools for achieving important organizational goals. In this respect, if

25

agency boards are viewed like any other task centered group, then executives should develop more skills that will enable them to improve their ability to work successfully with these groups. One area that executives should pay special attention to is helping board members understand what type of role they are being expected to play in the organization. Put another way, what is expected of a board member? Frequently, board members are unclear about what types of activities they should become involved in. Good executives must therefore devote considerable time to educating their board members as to what their roles are and can be. Another area that deserves attention by the executive is the initial recruitment of members. Dilemmas frequently arise around how important it is to choose people who represent important elements within the community versus choosing people who have specific skills or who are known to be task-oriented workers. Executives using this case study will be able to discuss these kinds of dilemmas as well as others and make choices about what types of people to recruit for the board based on their assessment of what the major purposes of a board are.

Finally, there are many devices that executives can use to manage the agency board successfully. Of major importance, however, is the periodic use of retreats or intensive planning sessions by the executive to help the board provide feedback about the future direction of the organization. Executives need to share the responsibility for strategic planning with their boards, and, if they do, the board will become an active partner in organizational change, not a passive or symbolic member of just another board. Executives, in the long run, must value agency boards and recognize their central importance to the functioning of a successful organization. When they understand their strategic importance more fully, then acquiring skills in board development will become more meaningful.

The Santa Clara County Elder Care Program

Santa Clara County is an area of about 500 square miles. Much of it had been farmland, but the county seat, Santa Clara, is now a bustling, growing city of 200,000 people (including its expanding suburbs). Two other Santa Clara communities, Redwood City and Cartersville, each have populations of about 50,000. The mild climate has made the area a desirable retirement location and almost 19% of the present population is over age 60. A recent study indicates that almost 70,000 of Santa Clara's residents fall into this category.

Social services in the several communities and the adjacent rural areas have barely kept pace with the steady growth of the population. The population is now ethnically mixed, in part as a result of several national refugee-resettlement programs and Santa Clara's geographical location astride the North-South migrant stream. About 12% of the Santa Clara population is black, 20% is Hispanic, and 11% is of Asian origin.

The economic base of the area is characterized by a combination of agriculture, agriculture service industries, light manufacturing and assembly, and a vacation and leisure business sector. Its county and city governments are generally well managed.

The Santa Clara Elder Program is a multiservice, multifunded organization that was founded 15 years ago by a small group of concerned citizens who wanted to provide leisure-time activities and nutrition services to the poor and frail elderly of the county. Originally a volunteer effort supported by contributions from churches and civic organizations, the program expanded as new federal funds became available. As the program grew, Clare Hanson, a widow with business-management experience, was asked to take over full-time direction of the program. The agency's services have now grown to include a senior transportation and escort service, a day-care center, a small Meals-on-Wheels program, and a modest homemaker-homecare program. The Santa Clara Elder Care Program has a staff of 15 and an annual budget of almost $800,000.

Ms. Hanson was well known in the community. The 10-person board of directors (most are from the original founding group) have been content to leave almost total control of the organization to her. Board meetings were perfunctory and served primarily as a vehicle for Ms. Hanson to report her activities. The program has received regular support from the Area Agency on Aging (AAA), the United Way, and the county board of commissioners. Two months ago, however, Ms. Hanson learned that she has a terminal illness, and she resigned as the head of the program. The board of directors was totally unprepared for this sudden loss of the organization's mainstay and immediately sought help from the executives at United Way and the Area Agency on Aging in trying to figure out what to do next. Both executives gave similar reports to the board of directors. They made the following points:

• With the impending impact of federal budget cuts, it was highly likely that fewer public dollars would be available in the future, and resource development should be a top priority and responsibility of the board of directors at Santa Clara Elder Care.

• The present board of directors was now very unrepresentative of the present ethnic makeup of the community. This situation could result in negative judgments from the United Way budget committees and the program committee of the AAA, if not corrected soon.

• Both executives stated very strongly that board enhancement and development would be the key factors in the agency's survival in the months and years ahead.

When the board met to review these recommendations, there was an atmosphere of hesitation and confusion. For years they had let Ms. Hanson handle all of the responsibilities and burdens. One board member, however, was both intrigued and challenged by the present situation. Tom Ewell, a relative newcomer to the board, is the manager of a local insurance company. Tom originally agreed to join the board at the behest of his aunt, who was one of the organization's founders. Active in the United Way and his civic association, he had a strong sense of civic responsibility and a commitment to community improvement. He had not been very active in the Elder Care Program, however, because Ms. Hanson had never asked for help, and the board meetings had been simply status-report sessions.

Tom now urged his fellow board members to recognize that rapid action was essential or the agency would flounder. After a discussion of the nature and scope of the tasks ahead, though, many of the old-timers—the founding group—stated that they could not devote that much time to the organization and they resigned. Only four board members remained, including Tom. Tom volunteered to temporarily chair this remaining group, now charged with the responsibility of reorganizing the board of directors.

Tom had a pretty good relationship with Amy Lowell, the executive director of Hospice, Inc., and he sought her advice. Tom's wife was a member of the Hospice board, and he was impressed with her enthusiasm, commitment, and involvement in the policy direction by board members of that organization. He was anxious to determine why the board was so different from the one at the Elder Care Program and how he might be able to incorporate some of Hospice's successful strategies into his own organization.

Amy shared with Tom the process of corporate planning and development used by Hospice. This process places strong emphasis on the leadership, stewardship, and trusteeship that human services organizations must receive from their boards of directors if they are to weather difficult times. After his discussion with Amy, Tom could see the relationship between organizational vitality and a board of directors that accepts responsibility for goal formulation, overall direction of the corporate process, resource procurement, budget approval, and organizational performance review. He gained a new understanding of the duties of an effective board of directors. After meeting with Amy, Tom was convinced that the situation at the Elder Care Program could be turned around, and he even became excited about the challenge. Faced with the task of rebuilding the board of directors, Tom convened a meeting with the other three remaining board members to bring them up to date, share his experience at Hospice, and ask for their advice.

The other remaining board members were:

- Carol Owen, a retired bank officer and founding member of Elder Care who is deeply committed to the organization. She has skills as a fund-raiser and an interest in resource development.
- Michael Starnes, who is a supervisor in the county's adult education program. He is also a member of the local Rotary Club and the Chamber of Commerce.
- Betty Reardon, who is a former nurse interested in the nutritional needs of the elderly. She was eager to take on more responsibility in Elder Care.

After some discussion, the four board members agreed that recruitment of new board members was doubly complicated because they were not clear as to the direction the organization was headed. Therefore Tom and the other three board members were unable to conclude what particular skills and characteristics should be required of new board members. Tom suggested that each of them consult with knowledgeable people in the community, as well as the present agency staff, and come up with a plan for the future of the organization as well as some names and sources of possible new board members. They would meet again in one week to prepare a preliminary statement of goals. Then they could use this statement of goals to identify potential board members. The new members could then refine these goals.

When the group reconvened the following week, they had collectively assembled the following information, some of which clearly supported what they had been told earlier:

- The stronger agencies in the community were characterized by boards of directors who were very involved in the development of agency policy.
- The growth of the elderly population had created an expanded need for services for the elderly in the county.
- Santa Clara Elder Care was very much needed in the county, but the changing character of the elderly population indicated the need for some different and possibly relocated services to serve emerging sectors of need.
- Resource development and fund raising was now a critical concern as federal funds are diminishing.
- The minority groups in the community had been systematically excluded from the governance of many social agencies, except for some tokenism, and Santa Clara Elder Care Services was indeed seen as a prime example.
- There were leaders in parts of the county and community where no one had ever thought to look for board member involvement in Santa Clara Elder Care Services.

The recruitment committee agreed that they needed at least 12 new board members who collectively could contribute to the achievement of future goals.

Questions for Discussion

1. How should an executive go about selecting a board? What criteria of selection should be used?
2. What are the major principles that should be followed by executives as they work with their board?
3. How large should a board be? What committee structure should be used? How often should it meet?
4. What criteria should be used to assess whether a board is operating successfully?

Pretest/Posttest

Listed below are statements that pertain to boards of directors in human services organizations serving the elderly. Please indicate whether you think the statement is true or false.

T   1. The board of directors establishes and maintains the legal or corporate existence of the organization.

T   2. The board of directors acquires and allocates the financial resources needed to carry out programming.

F   3. Development of agency goals should be the job of skilled professional consultants.

F   4. It is not necessary for the board of directors to reflect the population of the community that the organization serves.

F   5. Agency goals and objectives should be reviewed and revised every 5 years.

T   6. Board members can be recruited from many areas of knowledge and experience throughout the community.

F   7. In smaller agencies the executive director can take on many of the responsibilities of a board of directors and not burden the board with details of running the operation.

T   8. The qualifications necessary for a member of a board of
          directors for a not-for-profit organization are different
          in each organization.

3

Marketing Elderly Services

INTRODUCTION   Elliot J. Stern
CASE STUDY   Richard M. Hodgetts

Introduction

Today, managers of not-for-profit human service organizations are developing a sophisticated level of expertise in areas that were foreign to them a few years ago. Paramount among these is the ability to implement consumer-oriented marketing.

There are many reasons for this new marketing emphasis. Government and other third-party payers have steadily decreased their reimbursement levels and erratically shifted their payment mechanisms. Formerly, health care and social service providers were assured of continued sources of financial support from "paying customers" as well as for indigent populations. Now these same providers find their ability to serve charitable cases is based, in part, on "cost shifting" excess proceeds derived from caring for those who can afford to pay "out of pocket" or who have insurance coverage.

Also there has been an increase in the private-proprietary service network and a decreasing number of private-pay patients and clients. Organizations now realize they must compete for and attract new market segments—segments that traditionally were not part of their founder's original mandate.

Unfortunately the first response to rapidly changing market conditions by many human service organizations was to confuse marketing with expanded communication programs to the public. More public relations practitioners were hired; department budgets greatly increased; or inexperienced, in-place staff were given the title and additional duty of marketing director. The result was many institutions began extensive advertising campaigns believing that newspaper displays would create clients. Other facilities, wanting to be seen as taking an aggressive marketing stance, blindly jumped on the bandwagon when neighboring institutions began advertising their services.

Marketers now realize that effective public relations and advertising alone will not create sufficient demand and make any program a success. If there is no demand or if the public's needs are met elsewhere, extensive promotion programs are merely throwing good money after bad marketing plans.

Eventually knowledgeable marketers convinced their colleagues that marketing was not merely the introduction of a new service followed by a heavy advertising blitz. These erroneous tactics gave way to a more accurate definition of marketing and the rightful but limited role of public relations and advertising within that context.

Within the past decade successful providers have completely reversed their attitudes and beliefs about the delivery of services and products. Gone are the unsupported assumptions and attitudes that did little to prompt the organization's systematic measurement of the public's perceptions, needs, and wants. Instead, a consumer-centered philosophy has emerged.

Managers can no longer assume that their services and products, no matter how well designed or beneficial, will be accepted automatically by the patient/client who they now call "consumer." Not-for-profit organizations must accept the ultimate role of market demand in any given environment and then design programs the way the client wants them rather than in a way a manager thinks the social service system is supposed to work.

Once this centralized realization has been achieved, then the "nuts and bolts" of a marketing program can begin. Should existing programs be dissolved or modified, or should new ones be added to existing or new product lines? Should only clients who can afford to pay be targeted? Or are there ways of fulfilling original goals by opening new markets and, at the same time, finding new approaches to satisfy the unmet needs of an appreciative, current client population? These questions require in-depth demographic studies, environmental and market competition analysis, test marketing programs, and the establishment of sales and retention initiatives. The plan of action proposed in the case of the "Kings Manor Nursing Home" could prompt discussion of the development of these appropriate marketing schemes. How should questionnaires, seminars, focus groups, direct mailings, and telephone solicitations be used to design the product package? Will they confirm the original plan or prove it to be unwieldy, inefficient, or unnecessary?

Many other issues could be addressed. This case can point out the differences between marketing, promotion, and sales and determine what data are missing and what issues need clarification before the existing plan can be further developed. Most important, this case illustrates that a manager may no longer have the luxury of assuming that all consumers want their services no matter how good the services may be. They must develop knowledge about demand, environment, and program that makes their services and products appealing to the final arbiter of the marketplace, the consumer.

King's Manor Nursing Home

OPERATION FREEDOM

A private foundation was looking for a nursing home that would be willing to develop a model program for identifying frail elderly people living in an inner city area who could continue to live at home if home care services were provided. The foundation was willing to fund a 3-year, $200,000 per annum grant that would be used to provide services to these people so that they would not have to enter nursing homes. The philanthropist who headed the foundation explained her philosophy this way:

Many elderly people would like to take care of themselves and not rely on others. They believe in the good old American work ethic:

succeed on your own abilities and through your own efforts. However, some of these people are now quite old and they need some assistance. They are no longer able to do everything for themselves. They want to be independent, but they have reached that time of life when some outside assistance is needed. My $600,000 grant is designed to help these people maintain their current way of life at home. This is why I call the project *Operation Freedom*. We are providing them with some options, and hopefully helping them to continue living at home.

Roger and Betty King of King's Manor Home studied the five-page foundation grant application rules and guidelines. They felt that the philanthropist's ideas were not only quite logical, but also that King's Manor might be able to implement the project. Roger and Betty sat down and constructed a proposed plan of action. They estimated that seven people would have to be hired: four social workers, two case aides, and a project director. With this team, it would be possible to provide assessment and case management for 300 clients a year. Case management would include a wide variety of services including coordinating medical care, meals, transportation, personal grooming, homemaker help, shopping assistance, and financial services.

Most of the applications for the grant that were received were from people who had little, if any, experience in geriatrics. One was from a small print shop whose owner said that he was "looking for a chance to expand into other businesses." Another was from a group of five elderly people who wrote: "This program is designed for people like us, so who would be better suited to run it?" Unfortunately, the rest of their application indicated that they had no experience in administering a program of this nature.

The King's Manor proposal was the favorite of every program evaluator at the foundation. In particular, the evaluators were impressed by the fact that the Kings had identified the number of staff that would be needed, what each person would be doing, and what the various agencies and services were that could be called upon to supplement the foundation funds. "Obviously," the philanthropist told her program evaluation group, "these people know what they're talking about. Our grant would not be squandered with them handling it."

PROGRESS AND TERMINATION

Operation Freedom began in late 1982 and was scheduled to continue until late 1985. During this time period King's Manor was extremely successful in carrying out its mandate. At the end of both the first and second year, the program was evaluated by both the grant agency and state and local agencies. In all cases, it received glowing praise. One reviewer wrote:

This program has saved thousands of dollars per client per year. Without Operation Freedom it would have been necessary for most of these people to enter nursing homes. The project allowed the clients to continue their basic life style and provided them with a higher quality of life and more dignity than they would have enjoyed under any other circumstances.

Despite such fine reviews, the private foundation contacted King's Manor and told them that it would not extend the grant. The philanthropist wrote:

I believe that your success in this project has shown the value of projects such as Operation Freedom. The seeds have been planted and have borne fruit. Now I believe the program should be carried forward by either public or private funding. By now the state should be well aware of the value of continuing the project and, if there are any individuals who do not fall under current public programs, your nursing home has shown that it has the ability and desire to provide the necessary services. However, I believe now is the time for my foundation to bow out and look for other areas where we can make a similar contribution.

Of all of the people currently enrolled in the program, half were able to qualify for public assistance funding. King's Manor turned these files over to the provider service agency one month before the project terminated. Another 25% of the project's previous clients had resources to pay for these kinds of services and indicated that they would be looking for services to replace Operation Freedom. The other 25% of the people had some resources, but not enough to pay for all of the services they had previously received under Operation Freedom.

THE FOLLOW-UP PROGRAM

The director of King's Manor care services proposed to the Kings that the nursing home continue to offer services such as those offered under Operation Freedom under its own auspices. "We have the knowledge and the experience to stay in this area," the director explained. "It would be a shame to abandon this program just because the grant has run out. Why don't we look into a marketing plan and see if we can't make this program part of our permanent business?"

Roger and Betty thought the matter over very carefully and made a decision. They are sure that the 75 people who were previously part of Operation Freedom and can afford the full services will be willing to pay the Kings for these services. A brief estimate of costs indicates that for $120 a month, King's Manor could continue to provide assessment and case management in addition to coordinating the purchase of the necessary services for each respective client. This is how it would work: (a) each client would pay $120 to King's Manor on the first day of the month to cover the nursing home's fee for its regular services; (b) the cost of any additional services that may be required (transportation, house cleaning, assistance in bathing, food, etc.) would be paid directly by the client. King's Manor will oversee the entire process and ensure that both regular and additional services are properly delivered to the client.

After making a preliminary estimate of the expenses associated with continuing Operation Freedom, the Kings believe that they will need a total of 400 paying clients to break even. Some of these, hopefully, will come from the group of 300 that were included in the previous grant. The Kings believe that those who can afford the services will be very interested in having them continue the service.

INITIAL MARKETING PLAN

Before the Kings go any further, they want to develop a marketing plan. This plan will have four basic segments.

The first part will consist of identifying demand for this type of service. In addition to the 300 people who were originally part of Operation Freedom, there are many others who might be interested. The King's will contact various agencies, inform them of this service, and urge them to recommend people who might be interested.

Second, the Kings want to talk to the AAA people and see how much interest there is in funding this kind of program.

Third, they want to find out what similar services are being offered by other nursing homes or agencies in the local area and get an idea of how accurate their initial estimate of $120 per client per month is.

Finally, they would like to estimate all of the expenses associated with providing this service in order to more precisely determine how many clients they will need to break even on the project.

The Kings feel that the first step they need to take is to get as much exposure to potential referral sources in the local area as possible. Once they are able to estimate the initial demand, they then intend to see if they can stimulate additional referrals through a well-conceived promotional strategy. This, they hope, will get them 400+ clients. From here the program will spread through word-of-mouth and reputation and, hopefully, will build up to 700+ clients per month.

Questions for Discussion

1. Why is a comprehensive marketing plan a must for aging organizations?

2. What are the major components of a marketing plan?

3. What are the factors that make marketing of services successful?

4. What are the major principles of marketing that all good executives should follow?

Pretest/Posttest

Answer each question T or F (True or False)

T   1. Marketing has become a major concern for health care institutions in the 1980s.

F   2. The primary objective of a marketing program is to make a profit.

T   3. Marketing is particularly important in introducing new health care programs.

T   4. Effective marketing involves a determination of the overall costs associated with providing a particular product or service.

T   5. One of the most effective marketing techniques in health care is the defining of a market niche or target group to whom services will be directed.

F   6. The first objective of an effective health care marketing program should be to explain to the potential client why the program is well worth the cost.

T   7. Quite often effective marketing programs start by simply familiarizing the target market with information related to the new service that is being offered.

T   8. A well-designed marketing program includes a computation of the break-even point for the new service that is being offered.

T   9. In many cases, marketing programs are initially ineffective, and it is only after feedback from the marketplace that appropriate changes are made in the program.

F   10. Most health care marketing programs initially underestimate the market and then have to be adjusted to address the unanticipated demand.

4

Managing Change

INTRODUCTION   Cathy S. Kimbrel

CASE STUDY   G. Ronald Gilbert

Introduction

In 1980 Ronald Reagan successfully ran for President of the United States on a fiscally conservative platform. Privatization became the administration's battle cry that continues to this day to influence policy decisions at all levels of the human services delivery system. Integral to this approach has been the concept of decreasing citizen reliance upon the government for support of its human-service needs. The cutting back of federal dollars trickled down to the local service provider with cutback management being the basic administrative response.

In 1984 Governor Bob Graham created a Florida Committee on Aging to develop a "blueprint" for action to create and implement innovative aging services and strategies. Integral to the committee's report, called "Pathways to the Future," was demographic data relative to the aging population both at the state and national level. The report documented that Florida has the fastest growing elderly population in the country. It projected that between 1970 and 1990, Florida's over-65 population would increase by 20% and its over-85 population would increase by 203%. The report further stated that national studies reflected that 22% of the over-75 population suffered from at least one chronic condition that significantly limited their daily living activities. These statistics, coupled with the reported fact that 13% of Florida's elderly were determined to be poor, clearly reflected that the need for publicly supported human services would continue to increase into the twenty-first century.

This chapter hypothetically depicts an organization's response to the problem just described. Here we find a church-sponsored organization choosing to reduce over time its level of commitment to the provision of services to the elderly in its community. The goal is not only to make the organization independent of the church, but also to make it self-reliant. The problem with the second part of this goal is that a major component of the organization involves the provision of services to a low-income, minority population that cannot afford to pay for services rendered.

Human-service administrators will find this case study a valuable tool for discussing ways to manage organizational change. A critical component of the process is the management of employees who will be involved in assisting the organization in making the changes. This case study presents two distinct administrative approaches. Harry Tulsom is the newly hired executive administrator who recently sold a for-profit real estate development firm. As the chief executive officer of a for-profit corporation, he is used to approaching organizational change from an authoritative management style. Tom Anderson, on the other hand, was this human service organization's previous director who has agreed to continue on in the position of its administrator. He approaches organizational change from a participatory management style.

Discussion questions at the end of this case study will assist the reader in analyzing organizational change from the perspective of human needs and behaviors. Such an analytic approach is critical if human service administrators hope to succeed in their quest to maintain order in our ever-changing human-service system.

Part I

BACKGROUND

Brookline Elderly, Inc., is a comprehensive community-based service program located in Palm Beach County, Florida. It has been in existence since 1968, when it was developed by the Unitarian Church. It has two basic efforts: (a) The Brookline Retirement Center (BRC), which consists of 130 efficiency apartment units and 70 ACLF beds; BRC serves the middle- and upper-income citizens of the county on a private, pay basis; and (b) The Brookline Elderly Services (BES), which operates a low-income early-housing project, a home-delivered meal program, an adult care center, and a homemaker service program, all of which serve a local, low-income black population.

The church membership and its administrators want to reduce their commitment to these projects for a variety of reasons:

1. The projects have grown beyond their original intent and now consume too much time.
2. It is questionable whether the projects are appropriate for the church-based effort.
3. Community Development money and other governmental funding sources have run dry, and the economic viability of these services is in question.

A decision was made to establish Brookline Services, Inc. (BSI) as a separate not-for-profit corporation with a separate board and to bring in a new executive director to manage both Brookline Elderly Services (BES) and the Brookline Retirement Center (BRC). The new director's mandate is to make the two enterprises independent of the church and self-sufficient within 3 years. Harry Tulsom was hired as the BSI executive director. He is 62 years old and recently sold his business, a real estate development firm that specialized in building retirement communities. He has a 3-year contract as executive director. He understands that his contract will not be renewed at the end of 3 years.

Tom Anderson, the previous director of BES, has agreed to stay on in the position of administrator. The understanding is that Anderson will move into the position of executive director when Tulsom leaves, assuming that everything goes well. In the current setup, Anderson functions as Tulsom's deputy, and he is responsible for the day-to-day operations of both BES, a program that has been losing money and is a drain on the agency's resources, and the BRC, which is financially viable.

Most administrative-type policy decisions have been left to Mr. Tulsom's discretion and he has the full backing of the new BSI board.

Anderson understands that Tulsom, under direction from the board, is committed to taking a hard look at cutting programs that are inefficient and costing too much money. Due to the loss of federal community development funds, the housing project, which is part of the BES, is especially problematic. This project is targeted for the low-income community.

THE ANNOUNCEMENT

During the month of January, Tulsom spent a lot of time with Anderson and the executive staff, which consisted of the directors of finance, housing, maintenance, transportation, volunteers, public relations, planning, social work, Meals-on-Wheels, adult day care, homemaker services, and personnel. He met with them as a group four times. The group seemed to accept Tulsom well, even though many seemed concerned about the future. Up until this time, no mention of the planned cutbacks had been made to anyone on the staff by either Tulsom or Anderson.

In the first week of February, Tulsom suggested that Anderson "put the bean in the ears of the staff" about possible cutbacks. Anderson made his move at his next weekly staff meeting. He said that the new management was taking a hard look at the overall organization and that there might be some changes made. Anderson told the executive staff that he had been assured if any changes were made, they would not take place for at least 3 months.

Anderson's comment silenced the group. Since the change of status, (from the church to a corporate not-for-profit management approach) there had been many rumors that certain people were going to get the ax. Up until now, Anderson and Tulsom had done their best to assure everyone on the executive committee that none of them would be fired. The executive committee had even been encouraged to dispel any rumors about future cuts. Now the cat was out of the bag. There would be changes, and the overall impression was that Anderson and the new executive director were not being straight with their staff. It was obvious to Anderson that this was not a good time to go into the matter any further, so he adjourned the meeting by reminding everyone of his loyalty to each and every one of them. He also reminded them that the organization was entering a new phase in its growth and development, and that as managers and professionals they would be responsible for helping the organization make the necessary transitions when the time came to do so.

SPECULATIONS

On the following day two significant meetings were held. The housing staff met to discuss their concerns about the proposed changes. They were certain that their unit would be severely cut. They speculated that most of the cuts would be among the housing services and maintenance staff. The housing manager said, "If Tulsom were being honest, he would admit that he and this new nonprofit corporation have no interest in serving the poor black elderly." A maintenance worker added, "I don't want to say 'I told you so,' but if we were unionized, we would not have all of this to deal with." The social workers also had a meeting. They were concerned that the cuts would unduly hurt the low-income black community. The social workers reviewed the situation and after much discussion they agreed to attack the problem on three fronts. They decided to go to the Unitarian Church's Board of Directors and ask them to reassume the role they had previously played in managing the elderly programs. The social workers would argue that there was a moral issue involved here, and that the church still had a responsibility to see that the aged in the community were being provided proper care. They would also call for a meeting with Tulsom and Anderson and demand that any plans already made concerning the organization's future be immediately revealed and openly discussed. They also planned to contact the State Health and Rehabilitative Services agency to demand that a full investigation of the conduct of the management and its overall effect on the care of the aged in Palm Beach County.

By the end of the day, Tom Anderson had been fully briefed on what had happened at both of these meetings. He was concerned about the employees' discussion of unionization and the social workers' plan to go directly to the board of directors and the state HRS agency. He knew who the key players were in each group where the disruptions were occurring. He even knew which people among his own excellent informal network were being disloyal by playing the game from both ends.

Anderson called Tulsom that same night. He informed Tulsom of what had happened at the two meetings. Tulsom was very supportive of Anderson (he viewed him as a real pro), but he was furious with the other members of the executive staff who had let the news of future changes leak out to everyone in the organization as well as to the community. When Tulsom heard about the discussion of unionization and the social workers' plans, he said, "Tom, if they are that unprofessional, that militant, then fire all of them!"

Anderson sensed that Tulsom did not understand how to work with the professionals in the field of human services. Tulsom had good business sense but had no previous work experience in the not-for-profit human-services field. Tulsom did not view client advocacy as a positive role for the social workers or other professionals working for him. He viewed such practice as disloyalty. On the other hand, Tom Anderson had greater appreciation for the employees' positions.

Tulsom and Anderson agreed that Anderson should develop a plan of action and "nip this situation in the bud." Anderson did not sleep much that night; he had to have his plan in place by morning if he were to contain this thing before it turned into a major crisis.

Part II: The Next Day

By morning Anderson had thought through his plan of attack. He called an executive staff meeting. Once again he said that there were going to be changes in the future, but this time he pinpointed where these changes were likely to take place. He indicated that the changes did not need to be haphazard. "Together," he said, "they could manage to assure Tulsom, the board, the residents, and the employees that the management could meet their own needs without hurting the others." Anderson also let the executive staff in on what he had heard via the rumor mill the day before, but he did not discuss his sources of information. He asked them to further clarify the situation. He also asked for their ideas for resolving the situation. Anderson then telephoned Tulsom and informed him about what he had heard today and gave him his recommendations in a direct and forthright manner.

Essentially, both Tulsom and Anderson agreed that the best course of action was for them to convene a meeting with the executive staff and separately with each of their staffs in order to explain the Tulsom cutback plans and to identify what will need to be done so that the losses for all concerned will be minimized.

Following these meetings, several employee task forces were organized to help smooth the way for the changes planned.

Part III: A Few Weeks Later

Anderson's plan to be direct with the staff and to create mechanisms through which the transition from the present structure to that desired by Tulsom and the new board has moved along well. Due to the social workers' intervention, the board has assumed a stronger leadership role in the policy-making process of the agency. Much progress has already been made to identify another community sponsor for the low-income housing program and the Unitarian Church has agreed to continue to sponsor other programs for the black aged in the ghetto community. Part of the plan is for the financially viable Brookline Retirement Center to supplement the community programs and to eventually take them over from the church. Much to Anderson's credit, Tulsom has been very responsive to the suggestions made by the task groups, the executive staff, and Anderson. Although Tom Anderson's "team" approach to problem solving was alien to the thinking of Harry Tulsom, Tulsom has found it to be workable. Anderson has been able to retain Tulsom's confidence and, considering all that has happened, staff morale is good.

One nagging problem continues for Anderson. Two workers have continued to be strong, outspoken advocates for the elderly. They have been known to make negative comments about Harry Tulsom to representatives of local funding sources. Tulsom believes that this behavior is harmful to the overall morale of the agency. Furthermore, implicit in the employer/employee contract is the obligation of the employee to carry out the objectives set forth by the employer. "This is not the sixties," said Tulsom. "Any worker who does not carry out our objectives and who serves to undermine our efforts should be dismissed." Anderson does not think that what these employees are doing is right, but he feels that there is nothing that he or Tulsom can do about it. Both of the employees in question perform their job functions satisfactorily. Therefore Anderson has recommended to Tulsom that the situation be ignored. Harry Tulsom remains very upset with the workers. He feels resolved that such basic disobedience and disloyalty should not be tolerated.

Questions for Discussion

1. What are the major organizational barriers to change?
2. What types of strategies should executives use to deal with organizational barriers to change?
3. What process approaches to change should executives consider as they proceed?
4. What are the major principles of organizational change that should be followed by executives?

Pretest/Posttest

Listed below are statements that pertain to managing people in organizations. Please indicate whether you think the statement is true or false.

F   1. Although agency settings differ among programs for the aged, the personnel policies and procedures at each agency should be very similar.

T   2. When working in the private sector, one should have the same expectations for employee conduct as when working in the public sector.

F   3. When attempting to resolve technical problems, the participative or "team" approach to problem-solving through the use of task forces may not be the most effective approach.

T 4. When there is need for those who are required to implement a decision to be highly committed to that decision, a highly participative approach should be used.

F 5. The first step a manager should take when faced with a problem is to call his/her staff together and level with them. Then the manager should fully discuss the issue with the staff and let them help decide on a course of action.

F 6. What an employee does for the job is not a legitimate concern of an employer.

F 7. A manager should first identify the underlying causes of an organizational problem before attempting to resolve it.

F 8. Managing people of different professional and ethnic identities is a complex task that requires a manager to realize that everyone cannot be expected to share common organizational values and objectives.

5

Fiscal Accountability

INTRODUCTION Milan J. Dluhy

CASE STUDY Richard M. Hodgetts

Introduction

One of the major features of most nonprofit, voluntary organizations is their reliance on multiple sources of funds. It is the exception today to have an organization with a single source of funding. Some organizations may even have as many as 10 or 15 different sources of funds. One of the major difficulties presented to the executive who is in charge of an organization that has a number of sources of funds is the differing procedures and practices used by the different funding sources. For example, funding sources often require different types of documentation for accountability purposes. They may have different turn-around times for reimbursing the organization, they may have strict policies as to what they will reimburse for, or they may require periodic justification materials in order to continue funding a program or a service. All of these practices can lead to recurring cash-flow problems for the executive. This case examines the issue of cash-flow problems, as well as illustrating the things organizations can do to overcome this type of problem.

In recent years multisource funding in the aging field has become a common phenomenon. On the one hand, executives are being encouraged to expand their program and service offerings, while, at the same time, they are being asked to be more accountable for the spending of their funds. What often occurs is that an organization may have money in one account that is earmarked for a certain service, but the executive cannot use the money to pay for the expenses of another program or service where the funding source has been slow to reimburse the organization. Thus executives may have bills for one service but no money to pay for these bills, while at the same time, they may have money for another service, but the bills have not come in yet. Interfund borrowing and commingling of accounts are examples of questionable accounting practices. So what can the executive do?

This case provides the executive with insight into the strategies that can be used to deal with cash-flow problems and other problems created when organizations have multiple sources of funds. In time, adroit executives learn the wisdom of *rainy day* or *contingency funds* that are flexible and can be used to compensate for the variations in funding practices of the different funding sources over which an organization may have little or no control.

Funding for Food

BACKGROUND

The Waldren Group is a multiservice, multifunded elderly service organization in Indian River County. The group was formed in 1975 by a dozen senior citizens who had moved to the state in the early 1970s and settled into condominiums and apartments on the Intercoastal Waterway. Most of the group were retired business people who felt that not enough was being done to assist senior citizens. As a result the group decided to start a lobbying effort to raise the consciousness of city and county officials regarding the types of services they felt were needed.

The first thing they did was hold a mass meeting of all senior citizens in their respective condos. Then they held similar meetings in other condos and sponsored a countywide, all-day meeting called "For Senior Citizens Only." The purpose of these meetings was to get the retired community to speak out and identify those needs that it wanted the local community to address.

In all, there were more than 175 different activities, programs, or projects identified by the senior citizens. To address these concerns, the Waldren Group, which was named after their spokesperson, Bill Waldren, concentrated its efforts on two fronts. First, the group began lobbying efforts using the results of its senior-citizen meetings to persuade local agencies and government officials to direct more money into care and assistance for the elderly. Second, the businesspeople in the group contacted their previous employers and asked for assistance in providing some of these services. "I told my old chief executive officer (CEO) that something had to be done and done fast," Bill Waldren later explained.

The best way to do it was to raise some private-enterprise funds, underwrite a couple of projects, and show the senior citizens in this area that the Waldren Group could deliver. The CEO gave me a $10,000 grant and renewed it for 3 years running. The other guys in the group raised a total of $37,750, and we were off to a running start.

Some of these funds were used to buy new benches beside bus stops and to provide more programming for older people at the local recreation centers. Other monies were used for self-help programs for the elderly. The funds were also used to open an office, and a small staff was hired. The purpose of opening the office was to develop an advocate group composed of the retired citizens in the immediate area.

THE AGENCY'S EARLY YEARS

In 1978 the Waldren Group was incorporated as a nonprofit agency. Officers were elected, and a board of directors was formed. Bill Waldren was elected to head the agency and remained in that position until last year, at which time he stepped down in favor of a younger person.

From 1978 until Bill's departure, the group was involved in a series of state and local programs for the elderly. During this period the group evolved into an operating agency with an executive director, an assistant director, a bookkeeper, and a direct-service staff of 15 people. In 1986 the agency was operating through eight contracts, including Older American Act money, United Way funds, Community Care for the Elderly funds through the State of Florida, several direct grants from local municipalities within the county, and a CETA- funded training grant for older displaced homemakers. Their services included senior transportation and escorts, Title V employment, information, and referral services, homemaker and chore services, and home-delivered meals. They also operated two senior centers and one adult day-care program. The agency budget had grown to $3.7 million through these diversified funding sources, and some 1,900 older people in the county were receiving direct services through one or more of these programs. Although there were episodes of cash-flow problems during this period of expansion, the agency's fiscal and management staff had juggled the diverse funding sources and had been able to continue all services without disruption. While the agency was accountable to eight funding sources governed by a total of three different fiscal years, the auditing and control procedures of the funders were very sporadic and the council was generally able to get its money even when certain records were not available. Because of major problems in the CETA program and cases of fiscal mismanagement, fiscal monitoring and auditing are now much tighter.

In addition, because of his contacts with business, Bill was always able to get a loan at a local bank to cover any overdrafts. The loan was always repaid the minute the program funding was straightened out. The business that backed Bill's loan always paid the interest on the bank note since government funds cannot be used for interest.

In retrospect, Bill's ability to rely upon external funding help was both an advantage and a disadvantage. On the positive side, the agency never had to worry about cash-flow problems. On the negative side, the agency did not work very hard to develop strategies for dealing with cash shortages.

THE MEALS-ON-WHEELS PROGRAM

Three years ago Waldren received a county contract to provide hot meals to 412 elderly people. The contract calls for meal delivery five days a week, Monday through Friday. There are also some shut-ins who are given additional meals on Friday that can be heated over the weekend, thus ensuring that they have at least one balanced meal a day. The unit cost per meal is $2.97, and the total contract is for $325,000 for direct food expense and $65,000 for administrative, delivery, and out-of-pocket expenses.

The agency contacted the county 90 days before the current contract was scheduled to expire and expressed an interest in having the contract renewed for another 3 years. The necessary application for funding was submitted to the county within 7 days. Since that time the agency had its program review. Everything was favorable, and Waldren was led to believe that the contract would indeed be renewed.

As the old contract wound down to its last 30 days, Waldren still hadn't received any official communication one way or the other from the county. However, a staff coordinator who was close to the situation told the agency, "Don't worry. We've reviewed your application and everything is in order. It's just a matter of taking care of the paper work." This put the Waldren people at ease, at least for a while. When no formal action was taken by the last week of the contract, however, minor panic began to set in. Janice Beyer, the new director, put in a hurried call to the county. Here is part of their conversation:

Janice We're still waiting on a formal contract for the Meals-on-Wheels program. What's the status of our application?

County Employee Hey, no problem. As far as we're concerned, we're going to renew the agreement.

Janice Yeah, but when?

County Employee Just as soon as we can. You can't believe how busy we are over here. We've had our program review of Meals-on-Wheels. You know that.

Janice Well, when will we get a new contract?

County Employee Just as soon as the agency is able to schedule its advisory meeting to approve the refunding. This was supposed to be done last week, but the chairman's wife died the day before the meeting and the committee members wanted to go the funeral.

Janice Are you telling me that I should continue the program even though we don't have a formal contract?

County Employee No. I can't say that. But we don't want the meals disrupted. We'll get everything straightened out within the next couple of weeks and get caught up on the funding as well. If I were you, I wouldn't worry about the funding, and I'd find a way to keep the meals going.

Janice Okay. But I'd sure like a memo to the effect that you're authorizing me to continue.

County Employee You know I can't do that, but I really don't think you should be so concerned.

FUNDING THE PROGRAM

Because Janice was new to the agency, her immediate response to the phone conversation was to call a meeting of the bookkeeper and senior-level personnel. She explained the situation to them and suggested that they continue the Meals-on-Wheels program by taking some funds from other programs and, temporarily, use those funds to cover the unfunded meals expenses. The senior-level personnel agreed. "We've done this a few times before and it's worked out well. Let's do it again. After all, it's not our fault that the program is unfunded. We got our application well in advance."

The bookkeeper, however, expressed serious reservations. She was particularly concerned about the fact that an audit might be conducted and the accounts would not be in order.

The bookkeeper said to the group,

> last month an accounting audit of a multifunded program on Vero Beach turned up the fact that money from some accounts was being used to support other programs and all heck broke loose. Also, the more juggling we do, the more messed up things become. I think we're asking for trouble. What we should do is what Bill usually did: get a loan at the bank. This way we don't have to transfer funds from one program to another. Oh sure, we sometimes moved money around from one account to another, but that was only done in an emergency. Moreover the auditing and control procedures of the funders is getting a lot better. They used to be really lax and sporadic in their approach. But that's all coming to an end. I think we should borrow money rather than juggle accounts.

The senior-level personnel disagreed. They felt that the bookkeeper was making a mountain out of a mole hill. "Heck, we can't be blamed for someone else's error. Even if our books are messed up, they'd have to let it slide," they said.

Janice decided to try and keep all of her people happy. She called the local bank where Bill used to get loans. The banker told Janice that these kinds of loans were always personally guaranteed by the CEO of a large corporation. The individual who usually co-signed loans for the agency was out of town and would not be back for at least 2 weeks. Even if the corporate executive agreed to help out, the loan would have to wait until he returned.

Janice now realizes that her options are very limited, but she feels that she has to make a decision as soon as possible, certainly within the next few days. More important, she feels that she must develop a plan for dealing with these types of problems so she will be ready the next time.

Questions for Discussion

1. What are the major problems encountered in organizations that have multiple sources of funds?
2. What strategies can be used to overcome these types of problems?
3. What principles should executives follow as they manage an organization with multiple sources of funding?
4. Are there conditions/circumstances when an organization should turn down money from a funding source?

Pretest/Posttest

Answer T or F (True or False)

T   1. Multiservice agencies sometimes have multifunded programs.

F   2. In order to help with bookkeeping and ensure fiscal integrity, all service programs are funded on a July 1-June 30 fiscal year.

T   3. The latest state regulations prohibit borrowing funds from one program for use in another.

T   4. Due to contract funding problems, it is not uncommon to find programs being started up without the funding fully in place.

T 5. To reduce funding problems, many agencies get a financial advance from the appropriate county or other governmental agency to help them get the program under way.

T 6. Many agencies do not have a contingency plan for dealing with problems created by funding delays.

T 7. One of the major headaches in multifunded programs is keeping track of funds that are loaned from one program to another.

F 8. In recent years funding agencies have encouraged multiservice agencies to intermix funds when there is a shortage of cash in one program.

F 9. The best way to handle a cash-flow problem that is created by an administrative mix-up is to stop supporting the program. This will get the necessary attention and straighten the problem out in short order.

F 10. Recent government legislation is now making cash-funding problems a thing of the past.

6

Evaluating Program Effectiveness

INTRODUCTION Nancy L. Ross

CASE STUDY G. Ronald Gilbert

Introduction

Public and private agencies serving the elderly are being forced to become more accountable. Resources are becoming tighter. Demand for long-term care services is growing. The field has become more technical and sophisticated. Good public relations, while still necessary, will no longer be sufficient to ensure continued funding.

Evaluation is an important mechanism for providing accountability. What is evaluation? One author defines more than 100 different types of evaluations. Early literature claimed that a program could not be evaluated without written measurable objectives. However, written objectives often just measure process, such as the number of clients served or quality and quantity of services rather than outcome. Written or formal objectives can also vary substantially from de facto objectives. In the case of demonstration projects, objectives may have been overstated to obtain funding or written early in the project's life with the result that they are totally unrealistic. Basing an evaluation on such objectives could lead to the conclusion that a project was ineffective since the objectives were not achieved when, in reality, the project may have been making a significant difference in the lives of those being served. Although objectives can be written to focus on program results, objectives used to promote programs can miss important side effects. For example, an evaluation found that a project did meet its objective to return more nursing home residents to independent living. When other outcomes were included, the study found that this objective was achieved at higher public costs because the former residents used significantly more hospital days in addition to project services.

Recent literature suggests that to be effective, evaluation must be utilization focused. In fact, utilization is seen as the most important of four general areas for which professional evaluation standards have been written. The other three areas for which standards have been written are: feasibility, propriety, and accuracy.

To be useful, an evaluator needs to meet the information needs of key stakeholders. Key stakeholders may include the funding source, the service provider, workers, clients, other providers, advocacy groups, and the general public. Thus one of the first steps in any evaluation is to determine who the key stakeholders are and what their needs and interests are. For example, in the case study provided, it would be important to know the reasons a competing proposal was submitted so that the evaluation could address these concerns. Only after needs are identified can feasibility be assessed. Feasibility relates to what needs can be met within constraints of time, existing resources, and the political climate.

Based on analysis of stakeholder needs, a resulting evaluation could be broad or narrow in scope. It could be formative (i.e., focused on implementation issues such as managerial effectiveness or program performance); summative (i.e., focused on program results or client satisfaction) or both. It could even address the organization's ability to adapt to a changing environment, a possible issue in the case study. It could be qualitative or quantitative in approach.

In the case of demonstration projects, the focus of an evaluation is best determined at the start of the project. This allows more time for consensus to be achieved regarding the methods for measuring success. The greater the consensus, the more likely that evaluation will be seen as credible. It also allows ongoing systems to be designed so that evaluation is less intrusive. In other words, data for the evaluation can be collected as part of an ongoing project operation. Finally, it permits more powerful or conclusive designs to be used. In designing longer-term evaluations, care must be taken to ensure that the design is modified to reflect changing information needs. An effective evaluation can be designed at any time during the process. The types of issues that could be addressed adequately may be constrained, however. Whether an evaluation should be done internally or externally depends on a number of factors. Factors to consider are the types of issues to be examined, degree of political controversy, expertise within the agency, availability of staff time or resources to fund an external evaluation, and the need for ongoing evaluation. Unless the agency has an evaluation unit or trained staff, an outside evaluator can be particularly useful in the design stage.

Outside evaluations are generally seen as more credible or less biased to stakeholders, particularly those outside the agency. Disadvantages include higher costs and lack of familiarity with the program, which can result in conflicts between the evaluator and field workers in terms of any extra work imposed by the evaluation or failure to include key aspects. If institutional buy-in is necessary to implement findings, self-evaluation can be a powerful tool. With limited resources, collaborative efforts can be beneficial.

Selecting an evaluator is not an easy task. The type of expertise needed depends upon the focus. Furthermore the credibility of findings has been found to relate to stakeholder judgments regarding the evaluator. In addition to being technically skilled, evaluators must be seen by stakeholders as objective, open, and sensitive to the concerns of all stakeholders, not just the person who hired them.

In summary, evaluation is a complex endeavor. A variety of approaches are available. The most important ingredient is selecting an approach that will likely provide credible information to those who have a need or desire for it.

Evaluating Program Effectiveness

BACKGROUND

Ridgewood Elderly Services is a part of the Ridgewood County Department of Human Services. It serves a catchment area of 150,000 people. It has been in existence since 1965. Since its inception, Ridgewood Elderly Services has enjoyed strong political support. Ms. Agnes Townsend, the only director the agency has ever had, built the agency from scratch. It was through her efforts that the agency gained authorization and sponsorship from the county.

Townsend was able to gain support for the agency through her excellent connections in both the private and public sectors of the county. She was the former director of the United Way for both Ridgewood County and adjacent Jefferson County. When United Way started to become highly organized at both the national and regional levels in the early sixties, Townsend used her political clout to find a facility to house the services that she and her staff had been providing for the older adults. The Ridgewood County Commission provided the facilities and some indirect support. Ms. Townsend was able to relocate the federal grant she had for outreach services for the elderly to the county human services agency. (Jefferson County, population of 450,000, did not agree to adopt the program because its county commission did not want to compete with the local United Way.)

Since the program's inception, the Ridgewood County Commission has supported the elderly services program through indirect dollars and public praise for the agency's work. The program has been able to function more or less independently. Ms. Townsend was very adept at keeping her informal lines of communication open with members of the county commission and others who held political power. She was also able to obtain more than $35,000 in private donations each year for the past 3 years. Her fund-raising efforts were particularly helpful to the agency and the County seemed to use these efforts as a measure of the agency's success.

THE FOUNDATION GRANT

Three years ago the agency received a 5-year grant (3-year with minimum of a 2-year renewal, subject to contract compliance) from a large, prestigious private foundation. The grant was seed money for a demonstration of a new pilot project for the aged in Ridgewood and Jefferson counties. The project had four objectives:

1. To identify homebound elderly who are eligible for services but not receiving them.
2. To train caseworker aides to visit and assess the needs of the homebound.
3. To make appropriate referrals to provider agencies so that the isolated homebound would obtain necessary services.
4. To improve the quality of life for older adults in both Ridgewood and Jefferson counties.

The program was limited in scope. Although the target area was officially both Ridgewood and Jefferson counties, the program focused on three main communities within these two counties. The three main targets were the city of Halley, population 34,000, middle- and low-income rural farm whites; Retirement City, population 8,000, middle-class elderly, in Ridgewood County; and Garden City, population 22,000, primarily Spanish-speaking migrants, in Jefferson County.

The administrative structure included a director (Ms. Townsend, who worked half-time) and three supervising social workers: one in Retirement City who supervised nine caseworker aides, one in Halley who supervised five caseworker aides, and another in Garden City who supervised four Spanish-speaking caseworker aides. There was also a director of budget, an administrative assistant to the director, a director of transportation, and 12 transportation aides.

The local newspaper in Retirement City has published 20 articles about the grant project in the last 2 years. Most were human interest stories and all were very positive about the project. Several of these stories included photos of Ms. Townsend with other local dignitaries as they visited the elderly. The editor of the newspaper is Ms. Townsend's son-in-law.

THE CALL FOR EVALUATION AND
CHANGE OF LEADERSHIP

Three months ago the new director of grants at the foundation (the funding agency) requested that Ridgewood County supply its final (third-year) evaluation of this project. The evaluation was a stipulation made at the time the pilot project was first funded, and future funding was contingent upon this evaluation. Within 2 weeks of the receipt of this request, Ms. Townsend passed away. At the time of her death, she had not taken any action on the evaluation request. It was still in her in-basket on her desk at work. Dr. Jim Haynes, the newly hired director for the agency, learned about the request on his third day on the job.

Jim was hired through the county civil service process. He had once been the Community Action Agency director for Jefferson County. His recent graduation from the state university (where he took his Ph.D. in social gerontology) made him exceptionally well suited for the job, at least on paper. He had the formal qualifications that Ms. Townsend had not, but she had very strong political support in Ridgewood, which Jim lacked. He knew when he took the job that she was going to be a tough act to follow, and handling this evaluation request was the first real test of his ability to manage this agency.

In his effort to respond to the request for the evaluation report, Jack asked his administrative assistant to dig out the report so that he could take a look at it. The assistant, Agnes Bruise, didn't know anything about any evaluation. Jim then called a staff meeting with the budget director, administrative assistant, the three professional social workers, and the transportation supervisor. No one had any information about any evaluation that was to have been conducted for the funding agency. Jim informed the director of human services for Ridgewood County of his problem. Together they contacted the county comptroller, who confirmed that such a report was in the contract with the foundation. The County was required to submit the evaluation report to the funding agency within 60 days. The comptroller made it clear to Jim that a formal report was due, and soon. The funding agency understood the problem confronting Jim, but they needed the report in order to complete their own budget cycle on time.

THE FACTS

Jim immediately sought help from his staff to get this evaluation report under way. His communications with his staff and the funding agency revealed some interesting facts:

1. If the project was not refunded Jim would lose his job, because the County would not pay his high salary without the 50% match from the foundation.

2. The United Way in Jefferson County had decided to compete with Ridgewood Elderly Services for this project and had submitted its own proposal to the private foundation. The United Way in Jefferson County had also suggested that one of the three professional social workers reporting to Jim be named as director.

3. Record keeping in the agency varied. The office in Halley kept excellent case files with names, dates, services provided, and follow up. The office in Retirement City did not keep such records, but the supervisor's calendar was pretty well detailed as to both her travel and that of her aides. All travel had to be reported monthly in order for them to get reimbursed for personal expenses. The Garden City offices, located in Jefferson County, also had reasonably well-documented files. Though their process recordings were not very detailed, the basic contact sheets were like those recorded in the Halley office. It seems the supervisor in the Halley office wrote all of the case contact recordings for his case workers because the case workers were not proficient in English.

4. The main reason that Ridgewood County received the grant was because Ms. Townsend was a personal friend of the director of grants at the foundation and she learned that the foundation had some extra money that needed to be allocated. The director of grants has since been replaced by a former regional director of the federal government's Administration on Aging. This person did not have the same kind of personal relationship with Ms. Townsend as did the foundation's former director.

5. The evaluation could not be carried out by Jim alone. He was dependent on others to get the facts and figures for the evaluation.

6. The private foundation had planned to renew the county grant for another two years, and there was a strong likelihood that the grant would continue well past that time, but the recent application by the United Way of Jefferson County has made things more complicated. The foundation prefers to deal with one agency for both counties if possible. The death of Ms. Townsend has also seriously

weakened the relationship between the funding source and Ridge-wood County.

7. A line item in Ridgewood Elderly Services' budget targeted $14,000 for the implementation of the evaluation report. No money has been expended from this line item. The money can be moved to another line item and spent without special approval from the foundation.

Questions for Discussion

1. What are the major ingredients of a good evaluation? Or what are the major components of a comprehensive evaluation design?
2. What process considerations affect the successful completion of an evaluation?
3. What are the major principles of evaluation that an executive should follow?
4. Are there conditions under which an evaluation should *not* be performed? Why?

Pretest/Posttest

Answer each question T or F (True or False)

T 1. An objective is a criterion that should be used for pur-poses of program evaluation.

F 2. Program evaluation is a tool that is only useful in ap-plying for refunding.

F 3. Program evaluation is a rational management tool that has no bearing on organizational politics.

F 4. Program evaluation measures the effects of an agen-cy's activities, but does not focus on the activities themselves.

F 5. Program evaluation measures the activities of workers within an agency but cannot provide insight on the ef-fects of those activities on the agency's clients. These issues should be left to social science research and are not within the capability of an agency administrator.

F   6. If an organization does not have written objectives, it cannot be evaluated.

F   7. Generally, the evaluation of an agency's efforts should be conducted by outside experts who report directly to the agency head.

F   8. Staff members should not be permitted to evaluate their own project or efforts.

7

Interagency Cooperation and Conflict: The Dynamics of Coalition Building

INTRODUCTION and CASE STUDY

Milan J. Dluhy

Introduction

Increasingly, executives are called upon to join coalitions in the community in order to achieve collective goals that could not be achieved if the organization acted on its own. Coalitions are voluntary mechanisms for achieving a wide variety of political and nonpolitical goals in the community. Collective action by the coalition allows groups of organizations to pool their resources, share their expertise, and mobilize their respective memberships. In short, coalitions are useful vehicles for executives to use when the benefits derived from participation in the coalition exceed the costs of this participation.

The emphasis in this case is on how coalitions form, what their internal problems are, what kinds of strategies are used by

Author's Note: A revised version of this case study appears in Milan J. Dluhy, *Building Coalitions in the Human Services: Lessons From Practice.* Newbury Park, CA: Sage, 1990.

coalitions and, especially, what types of factors contribute to the success of coalitions. The theme that emerges is that coalitions are much like other groups in terms of organizational development. Coalitions need to be managed effectively, and many executives may often find themselves as leaders of coalitions or at least as active members of them. Therefore acquiring skills in the development and management of coalitions becomes another skill area worthy of attention by an executive.

While there are many internal and external issues that confront coalitions, the issue that very frequently challenges most coalitions regularly is the extent to which the membership of the coalition is willing to give their time to engage in blatant political activity. Many professionals who are members of coalitions are particularly troubled by being asked to engage in political activity that may conflict with their agency's interests, their own professional ethics, or their personal disdain for "politics." Nevertheless, coalitions are political by nature, and executives must always be mindful of when the costs of participation in the coalition become too high.

The Case

In 1982 and 1983 the State undertook a major study of the long-term care needs of the elderly. The underlying philosophy of the State was to preserve the autonomy and independence of the older person for as long as possible, and this philosophy was followed by the support and efforts of the State to keep older people in their own homes and out of very costly institutions. As long as the appropriate services could be provided, living at home was almost universally desirable as an alternative to institutionalization. Many of the service providers in Lime County came into contact with older people who needed support of some kind to remain independent. The service providers also recognized, however, that there were many "at-risk" elderly who currently had no contact with service providers or had contacts that were not helpful. In the latter case, some elderly sought services from agencies that could not help them directly and did not have the time or the ability to refer these people to the appropriate agencies. In short, many elderly people went unserved or were underserved by the existing agencies. There was a recognition of this problem within the community, and it was discussed in different forums such as the Council of Service Providers and a special Task Force on Long-Term Care organized by the Area Agency on Aging. Community awareness was high in 1985, but there was no organized and systematic attempt to deal with the problem at this point in time. In these early days, information sharing and the development of consensus about the problem took place informally and in a very ad hoc way, yet momentum toward solving the problem seemed to be gaining because of a fortuitous set of circumstances.

Because of severe budget constraints and the desire to keep people out of costly institutions, the State was eager to support and encourage community-based programs that would preserve the independence of the elderly. Also, the media and various advocacy groups continued to dramatize the plight of elderly people living alone in an alienated urban environment. Stories of people dying at home and being discovered by neighbors, scenes of elderly people not getting out of the house more than a few times a month, and stories focused on lonely and depressed elderly people who were not part of any social support system filled the local newspapers and received attention from the TV stations. Additionally, the federal government changed its reimbursement system to hospitals by adopting the DRGs, which, in turn, often forced elderly patients to leave the hospital and return home before their illnesses were over. Finally, insurance companies and HMOs were very eager to keep people at home and out of costly hospitals, and they continued to encourage more use of home-based services and less use of in-patient hospital treatment. All in all, these circumstances caused many community leaders to focus on the gaps in the service system that dealt with the "at-risk" elderly who wanted to remain in their own homes for as long as possible. Lime County, of course, which already had so many "at-risk" elderly and had a projection for even more over the next decades, became a prime setting for constructive problem solving.

BUILDING A PRESENCE IN THE COMMUNITY

In the summer of 1985 a concrete opportunity presented itself to Lime County. A major national foundation interested in the problems of aging decided to encourage demonstration programs around the country that would show how a consortium of community-based agencies could come together and work cooperatively to develop a coordinated and integrated system of services for those frail elderly "at risk" who chose to remain at home. Some of the members of the Council of Service Providers received notice from the foundation that money would be available for demonstration programs that could put together a consortium approach in their community. This opportunity stimulated a small group of service providers to call an informal meeting of agencies to see if there was any interest in applying for a grant from this foundation. Initial meetings were merely of an information-sharing nature. But after a few months, there emerged a working group of about 30 agencies that felt the community could submit a grant application to the foundation. A reason for coming together was apparent now. Each agency felt that if the grant proposal was written in a way that facilitated future cooperation, there might even be a way to improve their own respective services and thus enhance their agency's mission. Once consensus was reached on the objective of submitting a grant, the information-sharing process became more formal. Regular meetings were planned, minutes were taken, materials were sent out ahead of time, and a timetable for action was established. Up to this point, people had given their time sporadically, but once a formal agenda for the group was set, administrative tasks needed to be completed on time. One of the larger agencies in the community donated the time of two of their professional staff members to the consortium. These two people organized the materials, sent out the meeting notices, took the minutes, and, ultimately, wrote the grant proposal.

The consortium of agencies continued to meet throughout 1985. The focus agreed upon for the group was that a centralized information and referral system would be set up and each consortium member would be able to refer clients who they could not serve adequately. The I&R system named as a clearinghouse would then make a referral to the appropriate agency and, if no appropriate agency existed, they would lobby for the development of a new service in the community. Conflict in the group over what the clearinghouse would do was minimal. Most of the disagreement centered around how the clearinghouse would be organized, who would have administrative responsibility for it, and how it would be staffed. The primary incentive for participation of the agencies in the consortium to this point was that each agency would be able to use a centralized referral system for clients needing more or different kinds of services. The agencies would then be more efficient and, in some cases, they might even get more referrals to their own respective agencies. Because there was a clear-cut purpose, staff support and incentives for participation in the consortium, the coalition was quite effective. The proposal was submitted to the foundation, and there was much optimism that this networking approach would serve the community well.

The coalition of agencies called themselves a consortium only because the foundation limited applications for funding to consortiums. While there was a chairperson who ran the meetings during the time that the group was putting the proposal together, the group really only had a donated staff and no formal identity, no officers, no stationary, nor any of the other characteristics associated with more formal coalitions. Late in 1985 the foundation informed the group that their proposal would not be funded. For the next six months there were no meetings, and the agency people who had participated in the consortium never met as a group, even though some of them networked around other issues and concerns. The ad hoc effort had been successful, but now the group had no mission or purpose.

The chairperson of the group met socially one Sunday with two other members of the original consortium, and in their conversation they decided to take a stab at getting the group together again. The original group had a reunion early in 1986, and the results were very interesting. The consensus was that the group had enjoyed the process of meeting around the grant and they were proud of their product (i.e., the proposal). After some discussion, the group decided to meet monthly and to develop a new agenda for action. The chairperson of the original group urged the creation of a professional association of service providers. At a subsequent meeting the association became known as the Coalition for Independence and Autonomy for the Elderly, or CIA for short. By-laws were drawn up, officers were elected, a formal meeting time and place were established, and modest dues were collected from the members.

After much debate at an early meeting, CIA membership was opened up to individuals who had no agency affiliation. Within three months the membership of CIA went from 25 agencies to 30 agencies, and an additional 25 individual members joined the group. With 55 people and a budget of $2,000, CIA was in business. Initial meetings focused on getting the coalition organized and formalized and presenting information to the membership on budget cuts, sources of alternative funding, legislative changes, and new ideas about organizing home care programs. Attendance at meetings was good, and conflict was minimal.

In the spring of 1986, the president of CIA organized a small group to write a $15,000 grant proposal to a local foundation. The proposal was to fund six microcomputers for agencies who wanted to interchange their client files and records. This proposal was funded, and the six agencies developed a mechanism for improved transfer of clients and client information. Even though the proposal only represented a small amount of money to the six agencies who received support, it demonstrated to the agencies that joint action through the coalition could have immediate pay-offs for the members. This early success might be viewed more as a symbolic victory than a tangible one. The important thing is that it created incentives for continued participation by the members. A few weeks later, three members of CIA went to the state capitol to lobby for the budget that channeled money to home care programs in Lime County. Their efforts were successful, and they were very pleased when the State not only maintained the current budget level for the home care program, but also increased that level by 5% for the next fiscal year. Again, immediate results created more incentives for future participation by the members.

Finally, in the summer of 1986, the coalition organized a fund-raiser to help generate resources for CIA. The fund-raiser was held at a local hotel and was attended by 150 people. Many socially and politically prominent people attended this cocktail party and auction. This fund-raiser served not only to raise money for CIA, but it also gave members and their friends a chance to interact and network. This opportunity to socialize was an important incentive for many members to continue their affiliation with the coalition. The $5,000 raised by the event was earmarked for mailings, conferences, training, and travel. Practically speaking, the coalition had been able to attract members for a wide variety of reasons, and early successes had helped to set the stage for continued participation.

In the fall of 1986 membership in the coalition increased to 85 people. These newer members came from an adjacent county. About half of these were agency based, and half were independent members. The president organized a weekend retreat to develop an agenda for the succeeding year for CIA. The retreat drew 60 members, and it was agreed that seven committees would be established for the next year:

1. *Strategy Committee*—would guide the overall operations of the coalition and its activities.
2. *Talent and Recruitment*—would survey the membership to find out time availability and tasks that members would be interested in performing.
3. *Long-Range Planning*—would compile data on service needs, review the literature on "at-risk" elderly, and pursue foundation funding.
4. *Communications*—would organize a phone bank and all special mailings and would develop a newsletter.
5. *Special Events/Fund-raising*—would develop plans for receptions, fund-raisers, and annual board meetings.
6. *Media and Public Relations*—would develop press releases and stories for media.
7. *Monitoring and Oversight of Legislation*—would follow all legislature and administrative changes impacting on member agencies.

More important, the retreat established a clear-cut set of objectives for the coalition for the next year. After much debate, five objectives were established:

1. To develop brochures, handouts, and materials on CIA that stressed the fact that the coalition was focusing on the frail elderly, regardless of their income status. The coalition would circulate these materials throughout the community.
2. To encourage the State to set aside a proportion of their training dollars for paraprofessionals working in home care agencies of all kinds.
3. To approach the Lime County United Way for funding for social welfare agencies (not just home care agencies) that wanted to computerize their client records and referral mechanisms and to suggest that funding should come through a competitive bidding process open to all social welfare agencies in the county.

4. To approach a foundation to fund a detailed study of the needs for home care among the elderly in Lime County.

5. To strengthen all aspects of coordination between member agencies so that clients would be served better.

As 1987 began, CIA had a clear-cut mission and an operating organizational structure to implement their game plan. While some of the objectives did not appeal to some of the members, most members found at least one agenda item of interest to them. Two troublesome issues surfaced, however, as the coalition began to implement their strategy for 1987. First, even though the coalition had 85 members, the president always turned to three particular members for advice on how to run the coalition. Many members did not like this behind-the-scenes approach, and at one meeting they openly objected to this type of organizational management. The president argued persuasively that he would share power but needed a way to regularly access the members opinions and attitudes. A future meeting was set aside for discussion of proposals to remedy this situation. Second, as the agenda for action became more clear-cut, members were increasingly asked to actively lobby for the objectives of the coalition. Contacts had to be made with state legislators, local county commissioners, United Way board members, and other funding sources. Some members were uncomfortable with this type of aggressive marketing of the CIA agenda. Others felt just as strongly that without this aggressive marketing, there would be no reason for having the coalition since it would be unable to actualize its goals. Debate centered on "professional behavior" and what constituted appropriate behavior on the part of the members. The final meeting of 1987 was indeed controversial. One of the members designated by CIA to lobby in the state capitol for more training dollars for home care workers had sent a letter to all the members of the coalition, urging them to contribute to Representative Tom Riley's reelection campaign. At the meeting, one member said: "It is time to draw the line about what this coalition is all about. If I become a partisan, I will loose my self-respect, the confidence of my board, and the respect of my staff. After all, we are professionals and we need to remember that."

Questions for Discussion

1. What kinds of factors lead to the formation of coalitions among agencies and organizations in the field of aging?
2. What are the major elements of a successful coalition?
3. Describe the different types and forms of coalitions.
4. How can you keep a coalition going when it experiences a setback?
5. Can coalitions become too political? Are there consequences to the politicization of the members?
6. What are some of the lessons to be learned from this case? Think of a lesson as something that emerges from a positive experience that is worth repeating by a coalition.
7. Which is more desirable—an ad hoc coalition that accomplishes its objective and then goes out of existence or a coalition that becomes permanent but must increasingly manage internal conflict?
8. What types of incentives cause people to join coalitions?
9. When should an agency or individual withdraw from a coalition?
10. How aggressive should coalitions be? What image should they project to others in the community?

Pretest/Posttest

Answer each question T or F (True or False)

F 1. Successful coalitions can only be organized around "popular causes or issues."

T 2. Successful coalitions must have a clear-cut reason or purpose for being formed; they don't happen by accident.

T 3. Successful coalitions often have paid staff, formal rules, regular meetings, and independent resources.

F 4. Successful coalitions are always dominated by ideology rather than pragmatism.

T 5. Coalitions run the risk of becoming too political. If they do, members may resign.

F   6.   Coalitions can have only one mission at a time. Multi-
           mission coalitions are destined for failure.

F   7.   Permanent, long-lasting coalitions are the most desir-
           able. Short-term, ad hoc coalitions are less desirable.

T   8.   Members of a coalition have different reasons for join-
           ing, and there is no single reason people or agencies join
           a coalition.

F   9.   Effective leaders of coalitions operate behind the scenes
           rather than by interacting with the broader member-
           ship.

T   10.   Sometimes conflicts over the mechanics of running a
           coalition can cause as much conflict as the mission or
           purpose of the coalition.

Bibliography

Abels, P. (1977). *The new practice of supervision and staff development.* New York: Association Press.

Abonyi, G. (1982, September). SIAM: Strategic impact assumptions identification method for project, program, and policy planning. *Technological Forecasting and Social Change, 22*(1), 31-52.

Abramovice, B. (1984). Marketing long-term senior care services. *Health Marketing Quarterly, 1*(4), 5-18.

Adrian, C., & Press, C. (1968). Decision costs in coalition formation. *American Political Science Review, 62,* 556-563.

Albertina, R. M., & Bakewell, T. F. (1989, May). Allocating capital systemwide. Who gets how much and why. *Health Progress, 70*(4), 26-32.

Alexander, E. R. (1985). From idea to action—Notes for a contingency theory of the policy implementation process. *Administration and Society, 6*(4), 403-426.

Allen, C. V. (1985). A personal system for utilization review management. *Medical Group Management Journal, 32*(5), 14-21, 32.

Alperin, D. E., & Richie, N. D. (1989, August). Community-based AIDS service organizations: Challenges and educational preparation. *Health and Social Work, 14*(3), 165-173.

al-Swailem, A. R., & Ali, M. E. (1990). Functional health development model: A tool for planning. *Journal of the Royal Society of Health, 110*(1), 29-31.

Altschul, A. T. (1988, March). Nursing elderly people: The growing base of knowledge. *Aging and Society,* 85-94.

American Association of Retired People (1987). *A profile of older Americans.* Washington, DC: Author.

Amladi, P. G., & Caroselli, J. P. (1985). Using a microcomputer-based information system to manage and monitor departmental business operations. *Soft-Health, 3*(3), 56, 58-62.

Anderson, R. J., & Young, J. L. (1988, May). The religious component of acute hospital treatment. *Hospital and Community Psychiatry, 39*(5), 528-533.

Andron, S. (1987, March). Setting funding priorities in the voluntary sector: A case study from the Jewish Federation Council of Greater Los Angeles. *Journal of Sociology and Social Welfare, 14*(1), 55-72.

APA Task Force on Continuing Evaluation in National Health Insurance. (1980, April). The functions and structure of a national health insurance system evaluation component. *American Psychologist, 35*(4), 348-354.

Applebaum, R., & Christianson, J. (1988, July). Using case management to monitor community-based long-term care. *Quality Review Bulletin, 14*(7), 227-231.

Armstrong, R. P. (1982). Using agency coalitions to integrate service for children. *Social Work in Education, 4*(3), 59-68.

Austin, D. M. (1983). Program design issues in the improved administration of human services programs. *Administration in Social Work, 7*(1), 1-12.

Austin, M. (1984). Managing cutbacks in the 1980s. *Social Work, 29*(5), 428-434.

Austin, M. J. (1981). *Supervisory management for human services.* Englewood Cliffs, NJ: Prentice-Hall.

Avant, W. R., & Dressel, P. L. (1980). Perceiving needs by staff and elderly clients: The impact of training and client contact, *The Gerontologist, 20*(1), 71-77.

Aviram, V. (1979). Institutions and their changing environments: Structures and processes for adoption. Part I. *Administration in Social Work, 3*(1), 5-15.

Bacharach, S., & Lawler, E. (1980). *Power and politics in organizations.* San Francisco: Jossey-Bass.

Bahl, R., & Schroeder, L. (1984). The role of multi-year forecasting in the annual budgeting process for local governments. *Public Budgeting and Finance, 4*(1), 3-13.

Baird, L., Meshoulam, I., & DeGive, G. (1983, September-October). Meshing human resources planning with strategic business planning: A model approach. *Personnel, 60*(5), 14-25.

Baker, F. (1983, July). Manager and evaluator view of program evaluation. *Journal of Community Psychology, 11*(3), 213-223.

Baldwin, B. A. (1988, March). Community management of Alzheimer's disease. *Nursing Clinics of North America, 23*(1), 47-56.

Barton, M. B., & Schoenbaum, S. C. (1990). *Improving influenza vaccination performance in an HMO setting: The use of computer-generated reminders and peer comparison feedback.* American Journal of Public Health, 80(5), 534-536.

Bateman, T. S. (1980, June). Organizational change and the politics of success. *Group and Organization Studies, 5*(2), 198-209.

Beckman, N. A. (1981). Policy analysis for the Congress. In J. Tropman, M. Dluhy, & R. Lind (Eds.), *New strategic perspectives on social policy* (226-239). New York: Pergamon.

Beer, M. (1980). *Organization change and development.* Santa Monica, CA: Goodyear.

Behn, R. (1985). Cutback budgeting. *Journal of Policy Analysis and Management, 4*(2), 155-177.

Bella, L. (1982, Spring). The goal effectiveness of Alberta's preventive social service program. *Canadian Public Policy/Analyse-de-politiques, 8*(2), 143-155.

Benbenishty, R. (1989). Combining the single-system and group approaches to evaluate treatment effectiveness on the agency level. *Journal of Social Service Research, 12*, 3-4, 31-48.

Benson, D. K., & Marks, S. L. (1981). A needs assessment survival kit. *Southern Review of Public Administration, 4*(4), 425-447F.

Berger, B., & King, E. C. (1990, February). Designing services for the elderly. *Association of Operating Room Nurses Journal, 51*(2), 448, 450, 452-454.

Berman, G. D., Kottke, T. E., & Ballard, D. J. (1990, May). Effectiveness research and assessment of clinical outcome: A review of federal government and medical community involvement. *Mayo Clinic Proceedings, 65*(5), 657-663.

Berkley, G. (1984). *The craft of public administration.* Boston: Allyn and Bacon.

Bielawski, B., & Irwin E. (1984). Assessing program stabilization: An extension of the differential evaluation model. *Administration on Aging, 8*(4), 13-24.

Black, T. R. (1983). Coalition building—Some suggestions. *Child Welfare, 62*(3), 263-268.

Blau, G., & Boal, K. (1989, March). Using job involvement and organizational commitment interactively to predict turnover. *Journal of Management, 15*(1), 115-157.

Block, D. E., & Kurtzman, C. (1984, August). Family planning in a healthy, married population: Operationalizing the human rights approach in an Israeli health service setting. *American Journal of Public Health, 74*(8), 830-833.

Bloom, H. S., & Singer, N. M. (1979, November). Determining the cost-effectiveness of correctional programs: The case of Patuxent Institution. *Evaluation Quarterly, 3*(4), 609-628.

Bok, M. (1988, September). The current status of community action agencies in Connecticut. *Social Service Review, 62*(3), 396-410.

Botner, S. B. (1985). The use of budgeting/management tools for state government. *Public Administration Review, 45*(5), 616-619.

Bowlin, W. F. (1986). Evaluating performance in governmental organizations. *Governmental Accountants Journal, 35*, 50-57.

Bozeman, B., & Massey, J. (1982). Investing in policy evaluation: Some guidelines for skeptical public managers. *Public Administration Review, 42*(3), 264-270.

Bramston, P., & Harris, B. (1988, September). Quality assurance in residences for people with a disability. *Australian Clinical Review, 8*(30), 124-130.

Branch, L., & Jette, A. (1982). A prospective study of long-term care institutionalization among the aged. *American Journal of Public Health, 72*(12), 1373-1378.

Brazen, L. (1989, February). OR experiences are for student nurses. *Todays OR Nurse, 11*(2), 18-23.

Brekke, J. S. (1989). The use of orientation groups to engage hard-to-reach clients: Model, method and evaluation. *Social Work with Groups, 12*(2), 75-88.

Bresnick, D. A. (1983). *Managing the human services in hard times.* New York: Human Services.

Briar, S., & Blythe, B. J. (1985). Agency support for evaluating the outcomes of social work services, *Administration in Social Work, 9*(2), 25-36.

Brown, D. (1983). Administering aging problems in a federal system. In Browne, W. & Olson, L. (Eds.), *Aging and public policy* (201-219). Westport, CT: Greenwood.

Burgner, L. P., Zinober, J. W., & Dinkel, N. R. (1984). The impact of citizen evaluation review on community mental health center programs. *Evaluation and Program Planning, 7*(1), 57-64.

Bushore, M. (1987, April). Emergency care of the child. *Pediatrics, 79*(4), 572-576.

Cahill, B. F. (1986, November-December). Training volunteers as child advocates. *Child Welfare, 65*(6), 545-553.

Caiden, N. (1985). The boundaries of public budgeting: Issues for education in tumultuous times. *Public Administration Review, 45*(4), 495-502.

Calista, D. J. (1986). Linking policy intention and policy implementation—The role of the organization in the integration of human services. *Administration and Society, 18*(2), 263-286.

Campbell, D. T., & Stanley, J. C. (1966). *Experimental and quasi-experimental designs for research.* Chicago: Rand McNally.

Cantley, M. F. (1981). Strategic control for a United Kingdom regional health authority: A conceptual framework. *Behavioral Science, 26*(1), 1-28.

Capoccia, V. A., & Googins, B. (1982). Social planning in an environment of limited choice. *New England Journal of Human Services, Z*(2), 31-37.

Capwell, E. M. (1988, January). The state planning committee for health education in Ohio. *Journal of School Health, 58*(1), 12-15.

Carpenter, G. I., & Demopoulos, G. R. (1990, May 12). Screening the elderly in the community: Controlled trial of dependency surveillance using a questionnaire administered by volunteers. *British Medical Journal, 300*(6734), 1253-1256.

Carpenter, R. A., Boyenga, K. W., & Schaible, T. D. (1985). Evaluation of a prepaid mental health plan for business. *Community Mental Health Journal, 21*(2), 94-108.

Carpenter, S. S. (1986, January-February). Profit versus non-profit: Comparisons and considerations. *Home Healthcare Nurse, 4*(1), 18-23.

Carter, R. K. (1987, Fall-Winter). Measuring client outcomes: The experiences of the states. *Administration in Social Work, 11*(3-4), 73-88.

Casey, J. (1982). Reorganization in the eighties: An internal participatory model. *Public Administration Review, 42*(6), 576.

Chafkin, S. (1978, Fall). Community-based social services organizations. *Social Development Issues, 2*(2), 89-100.

Chalmers, J. W. (1990). Edinburgh's community drug problem service—A pilot evaluation of methadone substitution. *Health Bulletin, 48*(2), 62-72.

Chapman, J. J. (1983, May-June). Serving on the board of directors of a non-profit organization. *American Journal of Maternal Child Nursing, 8*(3), 173, 176.

Chase, P. A. (1989, June). Human resources management for a hospital pharmacy department. *American Journal of Hospital Pharmacy, 46*(6), 1162-1169.

Chisnall, P. M. (1979). The contribution of marketing research to health and welfare programs. *Administration in Social Work, 3*(3), 337-348.

Christian, J. (1980-1981, Winter). Using "outside resource people" in community-based organizations. *Journal of Alternative Human Services, 6*(4), 15-19.

Christian, W. P., & Hannah, G. T. (1983). *Effective management in human services.* Englewood Cliffs, NJ: Prentice-Hall.

Churchill, N. C. (1984). Budget choice: Planning vs. control. *Harvard Business Review, 62*(4), 150-164.

Clark, H. M., Burke, M. M., & Walsh, M. B. (1988, June). The linkage that worked: The Catholic University of America/Carroll Manor teaching nursing home program. *Journal of Nursing Education, 27*(6), 282-284.

Cooke, P. W. (1979). Human service planning issues for the 1980's. *New Designs for Youth Development, 1*(1), 4-6.

Cordray, D. W., & Lipsey, M. W. (Eds.). (1987). Evaluation studies. *Review Annual.* Newbury Park, CA: Sage.

Cornesky, R. A., & Anderson, J. A. (1987, May). Fund-raising strategies for the allied health professions. *Journal of Allied Health, 16*(2), 155-166.

Cutt, J. (1982). Accountability, efficiency, and the "bottom line" in non-profit organizations. *Canadian Public Administration, 25*(3), 311-331.

Davis, K. N., Boschen, M., & Miller, R. M. (1987, March). The development of a new service for older adults. *Health Care Strategies Management, 5*(3), 10-15.

Dawson, J. A., & D'Amico, J. J. (1985). Involving program staff in evaluation studies—A strategy for increasing information use and enriching the data base. *Evaluation Review, 9*(2), 173-188.

DelleFave, L., & Ragland, C. A. (1988, August). R.N. first assistants. A survey to determine the need. *Association of Operating Room Nurses Journal, 48*(2), 312-313, 315, 317.

DeRoos, R. L., Anderson, P. N., Berberich, N. J., Maugans, B., Omenn, G. S., & Rentos, P. G. (1988, July-August). Observations on work force and training needs for assessing environmental health risks. *Public Health Report, 103*(4), 348-354.

DiGiulio, J. F. (1983). Funding and the change process in family service agencies. *Social Casework, 64*(8), 466-472.

Dille, E. J. (1987, March). Mission statement translated into managerial, staff goals. *Health Progress, 68*(2), 68-70.

Dimock, M. (1983). *Public Administration.* New York: Holt, Rinehart and Winston.

Dluhy, M. (1981). *Changing the system: Political advocacy for disadvantaged groups.* Beverly Hills, CA: Sage.

Dluhy, M. (1984). Moving from professionalism to political advocacy in the human services—How to organize a successful statewide political effort in youth services. *Journal of Sociology and Social Welfare, 21,* 654-684.

Dluhy, M. (1986). Developing coalitions in the face of power. In B. Checkoway (Ed.), *Strategic Perspectives on Planning Practice.* Lexington, MA: Lexington Books.

Dluhy, M., & Rothman, M. (1986). The impact of Gramm-Rudmann-Hollings on Older Americans Act programs. North Miami: Southeast Florida Center on Aging, Florida International University.

Dluhy, M. J. (1981). Muddling through or thinking about the problem seriously: How to prepare policy documents, present information to decision makers, and maximize the impact of your advice. In J. Tropman, M. Dluhy, & R. Lind (Eds.), *New Strategic Perspectives on Social Policy* (240-256). New York: Pergamon.

Dluhy, M. J. (1981). Policy advice-givers: Advocates? Technicians? Or pragmatists? In J. Tropman, M. Dluhy, & R. Lind (Eds.), *New Strategic Perspectives on Social Policy* (202-216). New York: Pergamon.

Dobratz, B. A. (1988, January). Teaching complex organizations: A survey essay. *Teaching Sociology, 16*(1), 78-83.

Doherty, N. J. (1990). Resource productivity and returns to scale in school-based mouthrinsing programs. *Community Dentistry and Oral Epidemiology, 18*(2), 57-60.

Dorner, F. H., Burr, R. M., & Tucker, S. L. (1990, Winter). Hospital market share: The declining share of small players in the market. *Health Care Management Review, 15*(1), 11-15.

Downey, A. M., Greenberg, J. S., Vergilio, S. J., & Berenson, G. S. (1989, November-December). Health promotion model for "heart smart": The medical school, university, and community. *Health Values: Achieving High Level Wellness, 13*(6), 31-46.

Draper, R. J. (1989). The chronically mentally ill: Planning a future. *Psychiatry Journal, 14*(3), 463-466.

Droste, T. (1989). Marketing to seniors: Time, attention, and TLC. *Hospitals, 63*(3), 50.

DuBois, P. M. (1981). *Modern administrative practices in human services.* Springfield, IL: Charles C. Thomas.

Dunham, R. G., & Mauss, A. L. (1979, August). Evaluation of treatment programs: A statistical resolution of selection biases using the case of problem drinkers. *Evaluation Quarterly, 3*(3), 411-426.

Eadie, D. C., (1983). Putting a powerful tool to practical use: The application of strategic planning in the public sector, *Public Administration Review, 43*(5), 447-452.

Early, P. (1989). Target: Seniors. Older Americans flock to services they want and ask for. *Profiles of Healthcare Market, 1st Quarter* (33), 34-39.

Edinger, S. E. (1988). The Medicare and Clinical Laboratories Improvement Act of 1967 proficiency testing requirements and its relationship to the private sector. *Archives of Pathology and Laboratory Medicine, 112*(4), 357-362.

Edwards, R. L., Fearmen, S. R., & McGrath, M. R. (1986). The competing values approach to organizational effectiveness: A tool for agency administrators. *Administration in Social Work, 10*(4), 1-14.

Eisile, F. R., & Klundorfer, G. B. (1978). Forecasting for social services: A model for area agencies on aging. *Administration in Social Work, 2*(4), 401-410.

Elkin, R. (1985). Paying the piper and calling the tune: Accountability in the human services. *Administration in Social Work, 9*(2), 1-14.

Elkin, R., & Molitor, M. (1985-86, Winter). A conceptual framework for selecting management indicators in non-profit organizations. *Administration in Social Work, 9*(4), 13-23.

Enk, G. A., & Hart, S. L. (1985). An eight-step approach to strategic problem-solving. *Human Systems Management, 5*(3), 245-258.

Erickson, S. (1981). *Management tools for everyone: Twenty analytical techniques that are easy to learn and valuable to know.* New York: Petrocelli Books.

Eriksson, C. G. (1988). Focus groups and other methods for increased effectiveness of community intervention—A review. *Scandanavian Journal, Primary Health Care Supplement, 1*, 73-80.

Estes, C., & Newcomer, R. (1983). *Fiscal authority and aging.* Beverly Hills, CA: Sage.

Evashwick, C. (1984). Marketing services for seniors. *Health Marketing Quarterly, 1*(4), 19-32.

Evashwick, C. J. (1990, May). Older adults: A growing market for ambulatory care services. *Journal of Ambulatory Care Management, 13*(2), 1-14.

Evashwick, C. J., & Evashwick, W. T. (1988, February). Members program targets the senior market. *Health Care Strategies Management, 6*(2), 4-8.

Falek, J. I. (1986, October). Ensuring delivery of care as chosen. The administrator sets the environment. *Provider, 12*(10), 8, 10-11.

Fazio, L. (1987). Sexuality and aging: A community wellness program. *Physical and Occupational Therapy in Geriatrics, 6*(1), 59-69.

Feder, J., & Scanlon, W. (1989, Fall). Case mix payment for nursing home care: Lessons from Maryland. *Journal of Health Politics, Policy and Law, 14*(3), 523-547.

Feinstein, K. W. (1985). Innovative management in turbulent times: Large-scale agency change, *Administration in Social Work, 9*(3), 35-42.

Fernandez, T. (1984). *Oral communication for business.* Reston, VA: Reston Publishing.

Fielden, J. (1984). *Bottom line business writing.* Englewood Cliffs, NJ: Prentice-Hall.

Finlayson, W. C. (1984, July-August). CEO's challenge: Balance fiscal solvency, service to poor. *Hospital Progress, 65*(7), 66-72, 84.

Flora, J. A., & Farquhar, J. W. (1988). Methods of message design: Experiences from the Stanford Five City Project. *Scand Journal, Primary Health Care Supplement, 1,* 39-47.

Francis, A. M., Polissar, L., & Lorenz A. B. (1984). Care of patients with colorectal cancer. A comparison of a health maintenance organization and fee-for-service practices. *Medical Care, 22*(5), 418-429.

Frank, S. J., & Davidson, D. S. (1983, June). Ideologies and intervention strategies in an urban sample of drug abuse agencies. *American Journal of Community Psychology, 11*(3), 241-259.

Fraulino, L. J., & Simpson, B. J. (1989). The AIDS epidemic: Developing an institutional response. *Seminars in Perinatology, 13*(1), 44-48.

Freudenberg, N., & Kohn, S. (1982). The Washington Heights health action project: A new role for social service workers in community organizing. *Catalyse (US), 4*(13), 7-23.

Fritz, L. R. (1989, July). The mission statement: Framework for the hospital's strategic plan. The hospital's mission statement can be used to create a shared vision between the CEO and the board. *Trustee, 42*(7), 8-9, 25.

Fuller, R., Jordan, C., & Anderson, R. (1982, November-December). Retrenchment: Layoff procedures in a non-profit organization. *Personnel, 59*(6), 14-24.

Gamson, W. (1962). Coalition formation at presidential nomination conventions. *American Journal of Sociology, 68,* 157-171.

Gaylord, J., Jordan, R., & Kualness, M. (1986, February). Prescription: Office automation. *Journal of Medical Systems, 10*(1), 25-30.

Gelfand, D. (1988). *The aging network: Programs and services.* New York: Springer.

Genkins, M. (1985, Spring). Strategic planning for social work marketing. *Administration in Social Work, 9*(1), 35-46.

George, S. (1984). Challenges in marketing mental health senior services. *Health Marketing Quarterly, 1*(4), 69-76.

Gibelman, M., & Champagne, B. (1981). A consumer information system for staff development and training. *Journal of Continuing Social Work Education,* (1), 7-8, 23-26.

Giblin, P. T., & Poland, M. L. (1985). Primary care of adolescents. Issues in program development and planning. *Journal of Adolescent Health Care, 6*(5), 387-391.

Gilbert, G. R. (1984). *Making and managing policy: Formulation, analysis, evaluation.* New York: Marcel Dekker.

Ginsberg, P. E. (1984). The dysfunctional side effects of quantitative indicator production: Illustration from mental health care (A message from Chicken Little). *Evaluation and Program Planning, 7*(1), 1-26.

Girl Scouts of America. (1981). *Corporate planning in Girl Scouting.* (3rd ed.). New York: Author.

Glover, E. E. (1972). *Guide for board organization and administrative structure.* New York: Child Welfare League of America.

Gold, K. A. (1982). Managing for success: A comparison of the private and public sectors. *Public Administration Review, 42*(6), 568-575.

Goldstein, J. M., Cohen, P., Lewis, S. A., & Struening, E. L. (1988, April). Community treatment environments. Patient vs. staff evaluations. *Journal of Nervous Mental Disorders, 176*(4), 227-233.

Goodman, P., & Tate, N. (1987-88, Winter). Descriptive study of community based agencies servicing the elderly in one urban area. *Home Health Care Services Quarterly, 8*(4), 57-74.

Greenberg, J. N., & Ginn, A. (1979). A multivariate analysis of predictors of long term care placement. *Home Health Care Services Quarterly, 1*(1), 75-99.

Greene, J., & McClintock, C. (1985). Triangulation in evaluation-design and analysis issues. *Evaluation Review, 2*(5), 523-545.

Greene, J. G. (1988, April). Stakeholder participation and utilization in program evaluation. *Evaluation Review, 12*(2), 91-116.

Greenhalgh, L., & McKersie, R. B. (1980). Cost-effectiveness of alternative strategies for cutback management. *Public Administration Review, 40*(6), 575.

Greenley, J. R. (1984, August). Social factors, mental illness, and psychiatric care: Recent advances from a sociological perspective. *Hospital Community Psychiatry, 35*(8), 813-820.

Griffith, J. R. (1988, July). The mission of the well-managed community hospital. *Michigan Hospital, 24*(7), 43, 45-46.

Grizzle, G. A. (1984). Developing standards for interpreting agency performance: An exploration of three models. *Public Administration Review, 44*(2), 128-133.

Grizzle, G. A., & Witte, A. D. (1984). Evaluating multidimensional performance—A social judgment theory approach. *Evaluation Review, 8*(6), 777-800.

Gross, A. M. (1980). Appropriate cost reporting an indispensable link to accountability. *Administration in Social Work, 4*(3), 31-41.

Groze, V. (1986). Special needs adoption. *Children and Youth Services Review, 8*(4), 363-373.

Gruber, M. L. (1980). A three-factor model of administrative effectiveness. *Administration in Social Work, 10*(3), 1-14.

Gummer, B. (1980, Spring). A funny thing happened on the way to the top: Individual and structural determinants of career paths. *Administration in Social Work, 4*(1), 105-111.

Gutheil, I. A. (1985). Sensitizing nursing home staff to residents' psychosocial needs. *Clinical Social Work Journal, 13*(4), 356-366.

Gutknecht, D. B. (1982, Winter). Conceptualizing culture in organizational theory. *California Sociologist, 5*(1), 68-87.

Habel, M. (1986, Fall). A management blueprint for nursing staff development. *Journal of Nursing Staff Development, 2*(4), 134-137.

Haglund, B. J. (1988). The community diagnosis concept—A theoretical framework for prevention in the health sector. *Scand Journal, Primary Health Care Supplement,* 1, 11-21.

Hale, J. A. (1981, July). Where have all the dollars gone??? *Journal of Alternative Human Services,* 7(2), 15-16.

Halpern, W. I., Arkins, V., Mitchell, N., Freeling, N., & Healy, B. (1981, February). Continuity of mental health care to youth in the juvenile justice network. *Hospital Community Psychiatry,* 32(2), 114-117.

Hariston, C. F. (1981). Improving cash management in nonprofit organizations. *Administration in Social Work,* 5(2), 129-136.

Hasenfeld, Y. (1980). Implementation of change in human service organizations: A political economy perspective. *Social Service Review,* 54(4), 508-520.

Hatcher, M., & Rao, N. (1988, February). A simulation based decision support system for a health promotion center. *Journal of Medical Systems,* 12(1), 11-29.

Hatry, H. P. (1985, Winter). Program evaluation and client outcome monitoring for state and local human service agencies. *New England Journal of Human Services,* 5(1), 34-41.

Heath, L., Kendzierski, D., & Borgida, E. (1982). Evaluation of social programs—A multi-methodological approach combining a delayed treatment true experiment and multiple time series. *Evaluation Review,* 6(2), 233-246.

Heclo, H. (1979). Issue networks and the executive establishment. In A. King (Ed.), *The new American political system* (87-127). Washington, DC: American Enterprise Institute.

Heilman, J. G., & Martin, D. L. (1986). On the organizational theory of evaluation, economic and political constraints and the choice of an evaluation agent. *Administration and Society,* 18(3), 315-333.

Henley, E. C., Hodges, M. A., & Brooks, B. (1981, February). A working model for allied health clinical practice. *Journal of Allied Health,* 10(1), 23-27.

Hepler, C. D., Lucarotti, R. L., Rehder, T. L., & Slotfeldt, M. L. (1985, September). Improving patient-oriented pharmacy services: Panel discussion. *American Journal of Hospital Pharmacy,* 42(9), 1950-1956.

Hesterly, S. C., & Robinson, M. (1988, November). Nursing in a service line organization. *Journal Nursing Administration,* 18(11), 32-36.

Hillested, S. G. (1980). Applying strategic marketing. *Hospital Health Service Administration,* 25(Special Issue 2), 7-16.

Hinckley, B. (1979). Twenty one variables beyond the size of winning coalitions. *Journal of Politics,* 41, 192-212.

Hodgetts, R. (1980). *Administrative policy.* New York: John Wiley.

Hodgetts, R. (1986). *Organizational communication: A managerial perspective.* Orlando, FL: Academic.

Hodgetts, R. (1987). *Modern human relations at work.* Chicago: Dryden.

Hodgetts, R., & Cascio, D. (1983). *Modern health care management.* Orlando, FL: Academic.

Holmes, J., & Riecken, G. (1980). Using business marketing concepts to view the private, non-profit social service agency. *Administration in Social Work,* 4(3), 43-52.

Humphreys, N. (1979). Competing for revenue sharing funds: A coalition approach. *Social Work,* 24, 14-18.

Hsu, M. L., & Chen, S. C. (1981, Spring). An empirical study on employees' job stress. [Title appears in Chinese.] *Bulletin of the Institution of Ethnology Academia Sinica, 51*, 63-88.

Hughes, T. F. (1985). Financial impact of home health care on the hospital. *American Journal of Hospital Pharmacy, 42*(11), 2526-2532.

Hui, Y. F. (1989, October). Ideal models for social policies during the transitional period. *International Social Work,* 251-259.

Hulsebus, Fong C. (1988). Measuring corporate culture to ensure mission fulfillment. *Health Progress, 69*(9), 44-47.

Imo State Evaluation Team (1989, March). Evaluating water and sanitation projects: Lessons from Imo State, Nigeria. *Health Policy and Planning, 4*(1), 40-49.

Jahnigen, D. W., Kramer, A. M., Robbins, L. J., Klingbeil, H., & DeVore, P. (1985, July). Academic affiliation with a nursing home. Impact on patient outcome. *Journal of the American Geriatrics Society, 33*(7), 472-478.

Jerrell, J. M. (1982), Evaluating a management and organization development effort in mental health agencies. *Evaluation and Program Planning, 5*(2), 169-179.

Johnson, J. (1989, November 5). Managing cash in a crisis situation. *Hospitals, 63*(21), 26, 28.

Johnson, M. R. D. (1989, July). Health and social services. *New Community, 15*(4), 598-604.

Jones, B. D. (1980). The advocate, the auditor, and the program manager—Statistical decision theory and human service programs. *Evaluation Review, A*(3), 275-305.

Jones, D. (1980, Spring). Accountability and the politics of urban research. *Human Organization, 39*(1), 99-104.

Jones, L. R., & Thompson, F. (1986). Reform of budget control. *Public Budgeting & Finance, 6*(1), 33-49.

Kaldor, P., & Chambers, C. S. (1986, August). In whose interests? A case study of community work in a voluntary welfare agency. *Australian Journal of Social Issues, 21*(3), 183-196.

Kane, R. A. (1988, May). Case management: Ethical pitfalls on the road to high-quality managed care. *Quality Review Bulletin,* 161-166.

Karger, H. J., & Reitmeir, M. A. (1983, Summer). Community organization for the 1980's: Toward developing a new skills base within a political framework. *Social Development Issues, 7*(2), 50-62.

Kaye, E. M. (1988). The hottest new market: Seniors. *Hospital Entrepreneurial Newsletter, 4*(4), 1-2.

Kearney, J. (1986, September). A time for differentiation: The use of a systems approach with adolescents in community-based agencies. *Journal of Adolescence, 9*(3), 243-256.

Keith, J. M. (1984, November). Personalized care helps facilities compete. *Health Progress, 65*(10), 36-37, 61.

Kennedy, M. M. (1983). The role of the in-house evaluator. *Evaluation Review, 7*(4), 519-541.

Kerson, T. S. (1989, May). Progress notes. *Health and Social Work, 14*(2), 140-141.

Kessel, N., Hore, B. D., Makenjuola, J. D., Redmon, A. D., Rossall, C. J., Rees, D. W., Chand, T. G., Gordon, M., & Wallace, P. C. (1984, April 14). The Manchester detoxification service. Description and evaluation. *Lancet, 1*(8381), 839-842.

Kimberly, J. R., & Quinn, R. E. (Eds.). (1984). *Managing organization transitions.* Homewood, IL: Richard D. Irwin.

King, J. A. (1985, Spring). Building a mission statement—From the ground up. *Catholic Health Association of Canada Review, 13*(1), 7-13.

Kiresuk, T. J., Lund, S. H., & Larsen, N. E. (1982, February). Measurement of goal attainment in clinical and health care programs. *Drug Intel Clinical Pharmacy, 16*(2), 145-153.

Kirst, M. (1984). Policy issue networks: Their influence on state policy making, *Policy Studies Journal, 13*, 247-264.

Kneen, J. W. (1987). Planning for a healthier, more active senior market. *Healthcare Financing Review 41*(10), 25-26, 30, 32.

Knighton, A., & Heidelman, N. (1984). Managing human service organizations with limited resources. *Social Work, 29*(6), 531-535.

Knott, T. D. (1986, Summer). The distinctive uses of evaluation and research: A guide for the occupational health care movement. *Employee Assistance Quarterly, 1*, 43-50.

Ko, E. L. (1988, July). Mobilization of community energy in China. A case Illustration: Wah Nam Sai St. *Community Development Journal*, 170-175.

Kodner, D. L. (1981, Winter). Who's a S/HMO? A look at metropolitan Jewish geriatric center and its plans to develop a social/health maintenance organization. *Home Health Care Services Quarterly*, 57-68.

Korcok, M. (1988). Health care for seniors: A new and burgeoning market. *Canadian Medical Association Journal, 138*(4), 360-362.

Kotter, J., & Schlesinger, L. (1979). Choosing strategies for change. *Harvard Business Review, 2.*

Kuechler, C. F., Velasquez, J. S., & White, M. S. (1988). An assessment of human services program outcome measures: Are they credible, feasible, useful? *Administration in Social Work, 12*(3), 71 89.

Kunkel, B. E. (1981). Successful nurturing in residential treatment for abused children. *Child Abuse and Neglect, 5*(3), 249-255.

Kutza, E. (1984). Aging services and executive leadership. In F. Perlmutter (Ed.), *Human services at risk: Administrative strategies for survival* (165-179). Lexington, MA: Lexington Books.

Lamphear, L. (1982). *Shortcuts to effective on-the-job writing: How to achieve an immediate improvement in your business letters, memos and reports.* Englewood Cliffs, NJ: Prentice-Hall.

Lancaster, W. (1988, August). Marketing home health care to the rural elderly: From strategy to action. *Family and Community Health, 11*(2), 72-80.

Lang, R. H. (1980, October). Show me the way to stay home: A framework for long term care in the 1980s. *New England Journal of Human Services, Inaugural issue*, 39-50.

Langhein, L. I. (1980). Discovering whether programs work: A guide to statistical methods for program evaluation. Santa Monica, CA: Goodyear.

Lant, J. (1983, November). Creating persuasive fund raising documents for nonprofit organizations. *Caring, 2*(11), 22-23.

Lareau, L. S., & Heumann, L. F. (1982). The inadequacy of needs assessment of the elderly. *The Gerontologist, 22*(3), 324-330.

Larkin, H. (1989, November 20). Health care receivables financing comes of age. *Hospitals, 63*(22), 24, 26-28.

Latimore, J. (1986, December). A perspective on differential services in counseling: Altruism and likeness. *Journal of Sociology and Social Welfare, 13*(4), 823-862.

Lauffer, A. (1982). Assessment tools: For practitioners, managers and trainers. Beverly Hills, CA: Sage.

Lawrence, J.E.S., & Cook, T. J. (1982). Designing useful evaluations: The stakeholder survey. *Evaluation and Program Planning, 5*(4), 327-336.

Lee, J. (1988). Dental health promotion for seniors: The Toronto experience. *Canadian Journal of Community Dentistry, 3*(2), 29-30.

Leff, H. S., Dada, M., & Graves, S. C. (1986, February). An LP planning model for a mental health community support system. *Management Science, 32*(2), 139-155.

Lenraw, P., & Cowden, P. (1980). Human service professionals and the paradox of institutional reform. *American Journal of Community Psychology, 8*(4), 463-484.

Leung, J. (1986, January). Community development in Hong Kong: Contributions towards democratization. *Community Development Journal*, 3-10.

Levine, C. (1979). More cutback management. *Public Administration Review, 39*, 179-183.

Levitan S. A. (1977, May-June). Evaluating social programs. *Society, 4*(108), 66-68.

Levy, L. (1981). Reforming board reform. *Harvard Business Review, 59*, 166-172.

Lightman, E. S. (1982). Professionalization, bureaucratization in social work. *Social Service Review, 56*(1), 130-143.

Limongelli, F. (1986, June). The mission statement—a valuable working tool. *Australian Clinical Review, 6*(21), 60-61.

Liver, S. (1983). Speak and get results: The complete guide to speeches and presentations that work in any business situation. New York: Summit Books.

Logsdon, J. M., & Rubin, C. B. (1988). Research evaluation activities of ten federal agencies. *Evaluation and Program Planning, 11*(1), 1-11.

Lohmann, R. (1980). Breaking even: Finance management in human service organizations. Philadelphia: Temple University Press.

Loomes, L. M. (1985). Market strategies for an ambulatory geriatric health care program. *Health Marketing Quarterly, 2*(2-3), 63-73.

Louden, T. L. (1983). How to develop strategies to serve the aging health care consumer. *Trustee, 36*(7), 20-24.

Luft, H. S. (1982). Health maintenance organizations and the rationing of medical care. *Milbank-Memorial Fund Quarterly/Health and Society, Spring*, 268-306.

Lyles, D. C., Larisey, M. M., & Morrill, L. S. (1988, May-June). Health promotion for the elderly: A student experience. *Nurse Educator, 13*(3), 23-26.

MacNeil, E. (1985, Spring). The hospital mission statement: Quality assurance, whose responsibility? *Catholic Health Association of Canada Review, 13*(1), 14-19.

MacStravie, R. S. (1984). Marketing health services the engineering of satisfaction. *Health Progress, 6-5*(11), 35-37.

Macy, B. A. & Mirvis, P. H. (1982). Organizational change efforts—Methodologies for assessing organizational effectiveness and program costs versus benefits. *Evaluation Review, 6*(3), 301-372.

Maher, C. A. (1979, Fall). The 6 D's of management-oriented program evaluation in child and youth service settings. *Residential and Community Child Care Administration, 1*(3), 299-311.

Mandell, S. F., Duke, J. R., & Taliaferro, D. (1989, June). Advanced multi-attribute scoring technique (AMAST): A model scoring methodology for the request for proposal (RFP). *Journal of Medical Systems, 13*(3), 163-175.

Manson, S. M. (1989). Provider assumptions about long-term care in American Indian communities. *Gerontologist, 29*(3), 355-358.

Mark, M. M., & Shotland, R. L. (1985, October). Stakeholder based evaluation and value judgments. *Evaluations Review, 9*(5), 605-626.

Marlow, H. (1975). *Managing change.* London: Institute of Personnel Management.

Martin, K. (1989, October). Controlling the budgetary plan. *Nursing Management, 20*(10), 6.

Martinko, M. I., & Tolchinsky, P. P. (1982). Critical issues for planned change in human services organizations: A case study and analysis. *Group and Organization Studies, 7*(2), 179-192.

Matison, B. I., Ponomareva, S. N., & Muzichenko, N. S. (1986, July). Selection and training reserve managerial cadres: Formirovanie rezerva upravlencheskikh kadrov. *Sotsiologicheskie Isseledovaniya, 13*(3), 221-222.

Maynard-Mood, S., & McClinton, C. (1987). Weeding an old garden— Toward a new understanding of organizational goals. *Administration and Society, 19*(1), 125-142.

Maysey, D. L., Gimarc, J. D., & Kronenfeld, J. J. (1988, Spring). School worksite wellness programs: A strategy for achieving the 1990 goals for a healthier America. *Health Education Quarterly, 15*(1), 53-62.

McCurdy, W. B. (1979). *Program evaluation: A conceptual tool kit for human service delivery managers.* New York: Family Service Association of America.

McLaughlin, C. (1982). Strategic planning under current cutback conditions. *Health Care Management Review, 7*(3), 7-17.

Mendelow, A. L. (1983). Setting corporate goals and measuring organizing effectiveness—a practical approach. *Long-Range Planning, 16*(1), 70-76.

Meyer, D. R., & Sherraden, M. W. (1985). Toward improved financial planning: Further applications of break-even analysis in not-for-profit organizations. *Administration in Social Work, 9*(3), 57-68.

Milano, M. J. (1988, October). Hospital-based services for older adults: The myth of the elderly market. *Trustee, 41*(10), 8-10.

Miller, J. (1990). Access to interorganizational networks as a professional resource. *American Sociological Review, 45*(3), 479-496.

Miller, M. (1981, December). Community organization USA: The view from the movement. *International Journal of Urban and Regional Research, 5*(4), 565-572.

Miner, M. H. (1983, June). Preliminary contact with a mailed follow-up survey: Effect on rate of response of former mental health patients. *Evaluation Review, 7*(3), 385-396.

Moller, J., & Graycar, A. (1983). An eye for evaluation. *Administration in Social Work, 7*(2), 69-78.

Monk, A. (1978, Winter). Accountability criteria and policy strategies in direct service provision for the aged. *Journal of Gerontological Social Work,* 147-158.

Moody, M. L. (1990). Revising a drug information center quality assurance program to conform to Joint Commission standards. *American Journal of Hospital Pharmacy, 47*(4), 792-794.

Moran, T. K. (1987). Research and managerial strategies for integrating evaluation research into agency decision marking. *Evaluation Review: A Journal of Applied Social Research, 11*, 612-630.

Murnighan, J. (1978). Models of coalition behavior: Game theoretic, social psychological and political perspectives. *Psychological Bulletin, 85*, 1130-1163.

Nagel, S. (1984). Introspection deduction and guesswork in policy evaluation. *Evaluation Review, 8*(3), 413-424.

Neigher, W. D., & Schulberg, H. C. (1982). Evaluating the outcomes of human service programs—A reassessment. *Evaluation Review, 6*(6), 731-752.

Neuber, K. (1980). Needs assessment: A model of community planning. Beverly Hills, CA: Sage.

Newcomer, R., Harrington, C., & Friedlob, A. (1990). Social health maintenance organizations: Assessing their initial experience. *Health Services Research 25*(3), 425-454.

Nickens, J., Purga, A., & Noriega P. (1980). Research methods for needs assessment. Washington, DC: University Press of America.

Nielsen, C. (1989). Marketing the dental hygiene program. A public relations approach. *Journal of Dental Hygiene, 63*(7), 32.

O'Brien, J. E., & Wagner, D. L. (1980). Help seeking by the frail elderly: Problems of network analysis. *The Gerontologist, 20*(1), 78-83.

Oleck, H. L. (1980). *Non-profit corporations, organizations and associations.* Englewood Cliffs, NJ: Prentice-Hall.

Olfson, M. (1989). Psychiatric emergency room dispositions of HMO enrollees. *Hospital Community Psychiatry, 40*(6), 639-641.

O'Toole, L. J., & Montojoy, R. S. (1984). Interorganizational policy implementation: A theoretical perspective. *Public Administration Review, 44*(6), 491-503.

Palmer, J., & Sawhill, I. (1984). The Reagan record. Cambridge, MA: Ballinger.

Palmer, P. N. (1984, August). Federation adopts purpose statement . . . national federation for speciality nursing organizations. *Association of Operating Room Nurses Journal, 40*(2), 178, 180.

Palumbo, D. J. (Ed). (1987). *The politics of program evaluation.* Newbury Park, CA: Sage.

Pasmore, W. A., & King, D. C. (1978). Understanding organizational change: A comparative study of multifaceted interventions. *Journal of Applied Behavioral Science, 14*(4), 455-468.

Pauley, P. A., Choban, M. C., & Yarbrough, J. W. (1982). A systematic approach to increasing use of management oriented program evaluation data. *Evaluation Program Planning, 5*(2), 123-131.

Perlman, B., & Dobbin, D. D. (1984). System service provision and client service utilization in public sector human service organizations. *Journal of Community Psychology, 12*(1), 21-30.

Perlmutter, F. (1986). The politics of social administration. *Administration in Social Work, 9*(4), 1-11.

Perlmutter, F. D. (Ed.). (1984). *Human services at risk: Administrative strategies for survival.* Lexington, MA: Lexington Books.

Pestieau, P. (1989). Measuring the performance of public enterprises: A must in times of privatization. *Annals of Public and Cooperative Economics, 60*, 293-305.

Petrfreand, N. (1980). Community mental health center board development. Washington, DC: Government Printing Office.

Pillemer, K. (1984). How do we know how much we need? Problems in determining need for long-term care. *Journal of Health Politics, Policy and Law, 9*(2), 281-290.

Pint, R. M. (1988, April). Hospital consolidations: Expansion of mission or threat to ministry? *Health Progress, 69*(3), 41-44.

Pippin, R. N. (1980). Assessing the needs of the elderly with existing data. *The Gerontologist, 20*(1), 65-70.

Plambeck, D. L. (1985, October). The implication of board member composition for fund-raising success. *Journal of Voluntary Action Research, 14*(4), 60-66.

Plunkett, W. R. (1983). *Introduction to management.* Boston: Kent.

Poister, T. (1982). Performance monitoring in the evaluation process. *Evaluation Review, 6*(5), 601-623.

Poister, T. (1983). *Performance monitoring.* Lexington, MA: Lexington Books.

Poister, T. H., & McGowan, R. P. (1984). The use of management tools in municipal government: A national survey. *Public Administration Review, 44*(3), 215-223.

Popple, P. R. (1984). Negotiation: A critical skill for social work administrators. *Administration in Social Work, 8*(2), 1-12.

Price, R. H., & Politser, P. E. (1980). *Evaluation and action in the social environment.* New York: Academic.

Rapp, C. A. (1984). Information, performance and the human service manager of the 1980s: Beyond "housekeeping." *Administration in Social Work, 8*(2), 69-80.

Reichert, K. (1982). Human services and the market system. *Health and Social Work, 7*(3), 173-182.

Reinhard, S. C. (1988, September-October). Case managing community services for hip fractured elders. *Orthopaedic Nursing, 4*(5), 42-49.

Resnick, H., & Patti, R. J. (Eds.). (1980). *Change from within humanizing social welfare organizations.* Philadelphia, PA: Temple University Press.

Rice, M. (1988, June). Health promotion, education and community participation in the Americas. Reality or myth? *Hygiene, 7*(2), 7-11.

Riffle, K. L., Yoho, J., & Sams, J. (1989, December). Health promoting behaviors, perceived social support, and self-reported health of Appalachian elderly. *Public Health Nursing, 6*(4), 204-211.

Roberts, H. R. (1980, September-December). Meals for millions foundation: Limits and potential for international aid. *International Journal of Comparative Sociology, 21*(3-4), 182-195.

Roberts, M. (1983, Winter). Political advocacy: An alternative strategy of administrative practice. *Social Development Issues, 7*(3), 22-31.

Roddick, E. (1984). *Writing that means business: A manager's guide.* New York: Macmillan.

Rooney, P. (1985). *Business and professional writing: A problem solving approach.* Englewood Cliffs, NJ: Prentice-Hall.

Rose, S. M. (1986, September). Community organization: A survival strategy for community-based empowerment oriented programs. *Journal of Sociology and Social Welfare, 13*(3), 491-506.

Rossi, P., & Freeman, H. (1982). *Evaluation: A systematic approach.* Beverly Hills, CA: Sage.

Rossi, P. H., & Berk, R. A. (1981). An overview of evaluation strategies and procedures. *Human Organization, 40*(4), 287-299.

Rossman, G. B., & Wilson, B. L. (1985). Numbers and words—Combining quantitative and qualitative methods in a single large scale evaluation study. *Evaluation Review, 9*(5), 627-643.

Rothman, J., Erlich, J. L., & Teresa, J. G. (1981). Changing organizations and community programs. Beverly Hills, CA: Sage.

Rottleuthner-Lutter, M. (1989, October). Evaluation of a legislative measure. An example of the use of time series analyses in evaluating research: Evaluation einer legislatien massnahme. Ein beispiel fur den einsatz von zeitrehenanalysen in der evaluationsforschung. *Zeitschrift fu Soziologie, 18*(5), 392-404.

Rubright, R., & MacDonald, D. (1981). *Marketing health and human services.* Rockville, MD: Aspen Systems.

Rue, R. (1989, September 23). Resource management: Process and progress. *British Medical Journal, 299*(6702), 754.

Sager, A. (1982). Evaluating the home care service needs of the elderly: A research note. *Home Health Care Service Quarterly, 3*(2), 87-91.

Salvatore, T. (1985, Fall). The private non-profit home health agency: An exploratory essay. *Home Health Care Service Quarterly, 6*(3), 5-18.

Sandefur, G. D. (1983). Efficiency in social service organizations. *Administration and Society, 14*(4), 449-468.

Schaaf, S. V. (1990, March). An operational model of lifelong living. *Journal of Head Trauma Rehabilitation, 5*(1), 40-46.

Schaeffer, L. D. (1985). Health care marketing—A model for HMO services to the elderly. *Healthspan, 2*(6), 8-10.

Schick, A., & Hatry, H. (1982). Zero based budgeting: The manager's budget. *Public Budgeting & Finance, 2*(1), 72-87.

Schick, I. C., & Schick, T. A. (1989, October). In the market for ethics. Marketing begins with values. *Health Progress, 70*(8), 72-76.

Schinke, S. P. (1979, April). Evaluating social work practice: A conceptual model and example. *Social Casework, 60*(4), 195-200.

Schinnar, A. P., Kamis-Gould, E., Delucia, N., & Rothbard, A. B. (1990). Organizational determinants of efficiency and effectiveness in mental health partial care programs. *Health Service Research, 25*(2), 387-420.

Schmid, H. (1986). The changing role of management in human service organizations. *Human Systems Management, 6*(1), 71-81.

Schmid, T. (1989, July). Sociological education with a mission. *Teaching Sociology, 17*(3), 323-329.

Schneider, A. L. (1982). Studying policy implementation—A conceptual framework. *Evaluation Review, SS*(6), 715-730.

Schneider, A. L. (1986). The evolution of a policy orientation for evaluation research: A guide to practice. *Public Administration Review, 46*(4), 356-363.

Schwartz, A. Y., Gottesman, E. W., & Perlmutter, F. D. (1988). Blackwell: A case study in feminist administration. *Administration in Social Work, 12*(2), 5-15.

Sears, C. J. (1988, November). Organizational resources for the occupational therapist in the public schools. *American Journal of Occupational Therapy, 42*(11), 740-750.

Seidenberg, A. (1984, October). School nurses: Improve the reception and sharpen the image. *Journal of School Health, 54*(9), 363-365.

Shamansky, S. L., & Germain, L. (1987, February). The elderly market for nurse practitioner services. *Western Journal of Nursing, 9*(1), 87-106.

Shamansky, S. L., Schilling, L. S., & Holbrook, T. L. (1985, July-August). Determining the market for nurse practitioner services: The New Haven experience. *Nursing Research, 34*(4), 242-247.

Shayne, V. T., & Kaplan, B. J. (1988, December). AIDS education for adolescents. *Youth and Society, 20*(2), 180-208.

Sherman, E., & Cooper, P. (1988). Life satisfaction: The missing focus of marketing to seniors. *Journal of Health Care Marketing, 8*(1), 69-71.

Shittle, K. R. L., Gaulin-Kremer, E., Witzel, C., Keating, D. L., & Klaber, M. M. (1982). Staff development in a community-based respite program. *Child Welfare, ja*(3), 161-170.

Shulman, L. C., & Mantell, J. E. (1988). The AIDS crisis: A United States health care perspective. *Social Science and Medicine, 26*(10), 979.

Siegel, K., & Doty, P. (1978, March-June). "Advocacy research" versus "management review": "Nader's Raiders" and GAO on community mental health centers. *International Journal of Comparative Sociology, 19,* 1-2.

Sills, D. (Ed.). (1968). Coalition formation. In W. Gamson, *International encyclopedia of the social sciences* (pp. 170-179). New York: Macmillan and The Free Press.

Simms, M. D. (1989). The foster care clinic: A community program to identify treatment needs of children in foster care. *Journal of Developmental Behavior Pediatrics, 10*(3), 121-128.

Slotfeldt, M. L. (1985, September). Improving patient-oriented pharmacy services: What the director can do. *American Journal of Hospital Pharmacy, 42*(9), 1943-1947.

Smith, B. L. R. (1982). The nongovernmental policy analysis organization. In J. Tropman, M. Dluhy, & R. Lind, (Eds.), *New strategic perspectives on social policy* (217-225). New York: Pergamon.

Smith, D. L., & Bryant, J. H. (1988). Building the infrastructure for primary health care: An overview of vertical and integrated approaches. *Social Science and Medicine, 26*(9), 909-917.

Smith, J. E., & Black, B. L. (1987). Hospital diversification: How to involve the pharmacy. *American Journal of Hospital Pharmacy, 44*(5), 1059-1068.

Smith, N. L. (1985). Adversary and committee hearings as evaluation methods. *Evaluation Review, 9*(6), 735-750.

Smits, C. (1988, September). The development of an intake questionnaire for ambulatory care for the aged. *Tijdschr Gerontol. Geriatr. 19*(4), 167-168.

So, F. S. (1984). Strategic planning reinventing the wheel? *Planning, 50*(20), 16-21.

Sorensen, G. (Ed.). (1981). *Older persons and service providers: An instructors training guide.* New York: Human Services.

Southeast Florida Center on Aging (1985). Grant proposal. Cases in elderly services. [Submitted to U.S. Administration on Aging.]

Speltz, D. E. (1982). Hospitals must change missions and marketing to better serve the elderly. *Hospitals, 56*(13), 56-70.

Spence, H., Spears, M. C., Vaden, A. G., & Hoyt, D. P. (1982, August). Teaching effectiveness in coordinated undergraduate program in dietetics. Assessments of students, graduates, and program directors. *Journal of The American Diet Association, 81*(2), 151-158.

Starling, G. (1986). *Managing the public sector.* Chicago: Dorsey.

Stearns, N. S. (1986, January). CME mission statements. *Mobius, 6*(1), 62-69.

Stein, A. (1986). Between organization and movement: ACORN and the Alinsky model of community organization. *Berkeley Journal of Sociology, 31,* 93-115.

Stein, S. R., Linn, M. W., & Weiner, A. S. (1981, September). Effectiveness of a service workers' action team (SWAT) for the elderly. *Journal of American Geriatrics Society, 29*(9), 411-417.

Steinberg, R. M., & Carter, G. W. (1983). *Case management and the elderly.* Lexington, MA.: D.C. Heath.

Stemberg, C. W. (1981). Program evaluation and program management. *Public Administration Review, 41*(4), 480-487.

Stephens, B. (1989, April). Attracting seniors. Red carpet treatment works. *Profiles of Healthcare Market,* (34), 10-14.

Stevens, W. F., & Tornatzky, L. G. (1980). The dissemination of evaluation—An experiment. *Evaluation Review, 4*(3), 339-354.

Stevenson, W., Pearce, J., & Porter, L. (1984). The concept of coalition in organization theory and research. [Unpublished paper.] Irvine, CA: Graduate School of Management, University of California at Irvine.

Stewart, R. (1989, January). Studies of managerial jobs and behaviour: The ways forward. *Journal of Management Studies, 26*(1), 1-10.

Stoner, M. R. (1983, Winter). Citizen advocacy in the implementation of federal block grants at state and local levels of government: The California experience. *Social Development Issues, 7*(3), 8-21.

Strasser, S., Denniston, O. L., Apsler, R., Nguyen, T. D., & Schulberg, H. C. (1978). Pre- and post-planned evaluation: Which is preferable? *Evaluation and Program Planning, 1*(3), 195-202.

Straussman, J. D. (1986). Courts and public purse strings: Have portraits of budgeting missed something? *Public Administration Review, 46*(4), 345-351.

Strenski, J. (1985). Market place perceptions and the home care communication plan. *Caring, A*(g), 18-19.

Stretch, J. J. (1979). Seven key managerial functions of sound fiscal budgeting: An internal management and external accountability perspective. *Administration in Social Work, 3*(4), 441-452.

Stretch, J. J. (1980). What human services managers need to know about basic budgeting strategies. *Administration in Social Work, 4*(1), 87-98.

Stromberg, M. A., & Wholey, J. S. (1983). Evaluability assessment: From theory to practice in the department of health and human services. *Public Administration Review, 43*(1), 66-71.

Stroul, B. A. (1988, October). Residential crisis services: A review. *Hospital Community Psychiatry, 39*(10), 1095-1099.

Stroul, B. A., & Goldman, S. K. (1990). Study of community-based services for children and adolescents who are severely emotionally disturbed. *Journal of Mental Health Administration, 17*(1), 61-77.

Stuen, Cynthia (1985, Spring-Summer). Outreach to the elderly: Community based services. *Journal of Gerontological Social Work, 8*(3-4), 85-96.

Sturek, J. K. (1989, July). Point of service computer system and drug-use evaluation: Implications for pharmacy practice in ambulatory care. *American Journal of Hospital Pharmacy, 46*(7: Pt 2), 617-620.

Swartz, R. D. (1980, Winter). Shopping patterns of residents in Detroit are government-assisted senior citizen housing. *Michigan Academician, 33-344.*

Symington, D. C., & Weston, K. (1987). Eighteen years' experience with a community-based vocational rehabilitation program. *International Disability Studies, 9*(3), 106-109.

Terroir, P. (1981, April-June). Care of the elderly in Sweden: Les soins aux personnes agees in Suede. *Revue francaise des affaires sociales,* 171-190.

Thompson, R. W. (1981, April). A conceptual framework for psychosocial rehabilitation. *American Journal of Orthopsychiatry, 51*(2), 317-326.

Toseland, R. T., & Rivas, R. T. (1984). Structured methods for working with task groups. *Administration in Social Work, 8*(2), 49-58.

Trecker, H. B. (1982). *Administrative management for the human services.* New York: The Federation.

Trochim, W. M. K., & Davis, J. E. (1985, Winter). Computer simulation of human service program evaluations. *Computers in Human Services, 1*(4), 17-38.

Trochim, W. M. K., & Davis, J. E. (1986, October). Computer simulation for program evaluation. *Evaluation Review, 10*(5), 609-634.

Tropman, J. (1980). Effective meetings: Improving group decision making. Beverly Hills, CA: Sage.

Tropman, J. (1981). The relationship between staffer role and policy committees. In J. Tropman, M. Dluhy, & R. Lind, (Eds.), *New strategic perspectives on social policy* (pp. 185-201). New York: Pergamon.

Tropman, J. (1984). *Policy management in the human services.* New York: Columbia University Press.

Tropman, J. E., Johnson, H. R., & Tropman, E. J. (1979). *The essentials of committee management.* Chicago: Nelson-Hall.

Turem, J., & Born, C. (1983). Doing more with less. *Social Work, 28*(3), 206-210.

Vardaman, G. (1981). *Making successful presentations.* New York: Amacon.

Vass, M., & Walsh-Allis, G. A. (1990, Winter). Employee dependents: The future focus of worksite health promotion programs and the potential role of the allied health professional. *Journal of Allied Health, 19*(1), 39-48.

Velasquez, J. S., Kuechler, C. F., & White, M. S. (1986). Use of formative evaluation in a human services department. *Administration in Social Work, 10*(2), 67-78.

Viamonte, N. E., Pope, J., & Dishman, J. (1989). Baylor health care system: A case example. *Series on Nursing Administration, 2*(1), 89-100.

Vincent, R., Martin, B., Williams, G., Quinn, E., Robertson, G., & Chamberlain, D. A. (1984, February 25). A community training scheme in cardiopulmonary resuscitation. *British Medical Journal of Clinical Research, 288*(6417), 617-620.

Vinyard, D. (1983). Public policy and institutional politics. In Browne and Olson (Eds.), *Aging and public policy* (pp. 181-199). Westport, CT: Greenwood.

Vogel, L. H., & Patterson, I. (1986). Strategy and structure: A case study of the implications of strategic planning for organizational structure and management practice. *Administration in Social Work, 10*(2), 53-66.

Warner, R. (1977). *Social change and human purpose.* Chicago: Rand McNally.

96   SERVICES FOR THE ELDERLY

Washington, R. (1980). *Program evaluation in the human services*. Washington, DC: University Press of America.

Wasylenki, D. A., Harrison, M. K., Britnell, J., & Hood, J. (1984). A community-based psychogeriatric service. *Journal of the American Geriatric Society, 32*(3), 213-218.

Watkins, B. R. (Ed.). (1984). *Assessing needs in educational and social programs*. San Francisco: Jossey-Bass.

Weber, J. (1975). *Managing boards of directors*. New York: The Greater New York Fund.

Wechsler, B., & Backoff, R. W. (1986). Policy making and administration in state agencies: Strategic approaches. *Public Administration Review, 45*(4), 321-328.

Weinback, R. W. (1984). Implementing change: Insights and strategies for the supervisor. *Social Work, 29*(3), 282-286.

Weisner, S. (1983). Fighting back: A critical analysis of coalition building in the human services. *Social Service Review, 57*(2), 291-306.

Weiss, C. (1972). *Evaluation research*. Englewood Cliffs, NJ: Prentice-Hall.

Weissert, W. (1985). Estimating the long-term care population: Prevalance rates and selected characteristics. *Health Care Financing Review, 6*(4), 83-91.

Weissert, W. G., Cready, C. M., & Pawelak, J. E. (1988). The past and future of home and community-based long-term case. *Milbank Quarterly, 66*(2), 309-388.

Weissman, H., Epstein, I., & Savage, A. (1983). *Agency-based social work*. Philadelphia: Temple University Press.

Whitaker, J. M., Severy, L. J., & Morton, D. S. (1984). A comprehensive community-based youth diversion program. *Child-Welfare, 63*(2), 175-181.

Wholey, J. S. (1979). *Evaluation: Promise and performance*. Washington, DC: Urban Institute.

Williams, M. E., & Williams T. F. (1986, January). Evaluation of older persons in the ambulatory setting. *Journal of the American Geriatrics Society, 34*(1), 37-43.

Windle, C., & Paschall, N. C. (1981, Spring). Client participation in CMHC program evaluation: Increasing incidence, inadequate involvement. *Community Mental Health Journal, 17*(1), 66-76.

Wineberg, R. J. (1985). Pulling together. *Public Welfare, 43*(4), 37-40.

Wistow, G. (1987, Summer). Joint finance: Promoting a new balance of care and responsibilities in England? *International Journal of Social Psychiatry, 83-91.*

Withorn, A. (1981). Human service agencies and unions. *New England Journal of Human Services, 1*(4), 46-53.

Wolk, J. L., May, I. P., & Bleeke, M. A. (1982). Human service management: The art of interpersonal relationships. *Administration in Social Work, k*(l), 4-10.

Wood, J. B. (1989). The emergence of adult day care centers as post-acute care agencies. *Journal of Aging and Health, 1*(4), 521-539.

Wood, J. B., Hughes, R. G., & Estes, C. L. (1986, Summer). Community health centers and the elderly: A potential new alliance. *Journal of Community Health, 137-146.*

YaDeau, R. E. (1985). Competitive medical plans: Why be first? *Health Progress, 66*(5), 35-37, 66.

Yanay, U. (1988, February). Ideology and reality: Representation and participation in local service management. Evaluating the case of Israeli Community Service Centre-Matnas. *British Journal of Social Work, 18*(1), 43-56.

Yankey, J. A., Lutz, C., & Koury, N. (1986). Marketing welfare services. *Public Welfare, 44*(1), 40-49.

Yedidia, P. (1990, May). Outreach program for older adults: Implications and opportunities. *Journal of Ambulatory Care Management, 13*(2), 27-32.

Yin, R. (1984). *Case study research: Design and methods.* Beverly Hills, CA: Sage.

Ziegenfuss, Jr., J. T., & Lasky, D. I. (1980). Evaluation and organizational development—A management-consulting approach. *Evaluation Review, AL*(5), 665-676.

Zitter, A. (1988, December). Older population most diverse of all American age groups. *Healthcare Finance Management, 42*(12), 38, 40, 42.

Zitter, M. (1988). Positioning for success in the older adult market: Hospital as hub. *Trustee, 41*(10), 17-18.

Zober, M. A. (1980). A systematic perspective on the staff development and training evaluation process. *Arete, 6*(2), 51-70.

Zober, M. A., Supel, M. O., & Skinner, V. (1982). Action oriented training and evaluation: Motivation and measuring change in job performance as a result of inservice training in departments of social work. *Journal of Continuing Work, 2*(1), 23-27, 41.

Author Index

Subject Index

About the Contributors

Milan J. Dluhy (Ph.D., University of Michigan) is Professor of Public Administration and Director of the Institute of Government at Florida International University (FIU) in Miami. He has also served as Acting Dean of the School of Public Affairs and as Associate Director of the Southeast Florida Center on Aging at FIU. Prior to his present position at FIU, he held faculty positions at the University of Michigan and American University. His career includes working as a Senior Policy Analyst with the U.S. Department of Health, Education and Welfare and serving as a consultant to the states of Florida, Michigan, and Vermont, and to many local governments, advocacy groups, political coalitions, and nonprofit human-service organizations in the U.S. He has authored or co-authored six books as well as many other professional publications in the areas of social policy, political advocacy and coalition building, and housing the elderly and homeless. He is currently working on how local governments are seeking to accommodate the reality of scarcity in light of the increasing demands from citizens for public services.

G. Ronald Gilbert (Ph.D., University of Southern California) is Associate Professor of Management, College of Business

Administration, Florida International University in Miami. He is a frequent contributor to academic journals and has presented numerous papers at professional conferences. He has also developed a wide variety of training materials and has conducted many training seminars for managers in the public, private, and nonprofit sectors. Managing for change and the connection between participatory management and productivity are common themes in both his writing and training.

Richard M. Hodgetts (Ph.D., University of Oklahoma) is Professor of Management, School of Business Administration, Florida International University in Miami. He has previously taught at Indiana University, the University of Oklahoma, the University of Nebraska, and Texas Tech University. He has authored numerous books and other publications in the field of management, organizational behavior, and business policy. He has also consulted widely with both private and nonprofit organizations.

Cathy S. Kimbrel (Ph.D., Nova University) is Director of Special Services, Gwinnett County, Georgia. She has held a wide variety of administrative positions in the aging field, including a staff position with the State of Georgia Office on Aging, the Section Head of the Broward County (Florida) Social Services Division of Elderly Services, and the Program Supervisor of the Broward County Gerontology Program. Her expertise is in the development and management of mental health and social service programs for the elderly.

Sanford L. Kravitz (Ph.D., Brandeis University) is Distinguished Professor of Public Affairs at Florida International University in Miami. Formerly he was the Associate Director of the Community Action Program in the Office of Economic Opportunity. He has also held previous academic positions at Brandeis University and the State University of New York at Stony Brook. He has consulted widely with planning and advocacy groups in the aging and human services area and written numerous papers and reports on community development and social change.

Martha B. Pelaez (Ph.D., Tulane University) is Associate Director, Southeast Florida Center on Aging, Florida International University in Miami. Previously, she was on the faculty and also served as a department chair at Xavier University, New Orleans. She has made numerous presentations at professional conferences in the aging field, directed a wide variety of research and training projects at the Southeast Florida Center on Aging, and consulted regularly with organizations in the aging network. She was the project director of the U.S. Administration on Aging fund grant, which developed the case studies used in this book. Her area of specialization in the aging field is ethics and the delivery of health and human services to terminally ill or extremely frail older people.

Nancy L. Ross (Ph.D., Florida State University) is a Social Science Analyst, U.S. General Accounting Office, Washington, DC. Formerly she was Supervisor, Office of Evaluation and Management Review, Florida Department of Health and Rehabilitative Services. Her areas of special interest are program evaluation and policy research methods and the development of needs assessments techniques for the elderly service recipient.

Max B. Rothman (J.D., University of Michigan) is Executive Director of the Southeast Florida Center on Aging, Florida International University in Miami. He has held other administrative positions, including the Director of the Florida Long Term Care Study Project, District Administrator of the Florida Department of Health and Rehabilitative Services for Dade and Monroe Counties, and Director of the Legal Aid Society of Metropolitan Denver. He has authored or co-authored numerous research reports and studies on the problems of the elderly in Florida and is currently directing a study that is projecting the needs of Florida's older population to the years 1995 and 2000.

Elliot J. Stern (M.A., University of Michigan) is Associate Executive Director, Miami Jewish Home and Hospital for the Aged. Previously, he was the Director, Division of Government Policy,

American Planning Association; the Minority Staff Director, Subcommittee on Health and Long Term Care, U.S. House Select Committee on Aging; and the Director of Education and Research, Group Health Association of America. He has also developed and managed a number of nationally recognized community-based care programs for the elderly in Miami.